MW01379528

BURMESE REFUGEES

Letters from
the
Thai-Burma Border

edited by

T F Rhoden
&
T L S Rhoden

Burmese Refugees, Letters from the Thai-Burma Border published by Digital Lycanthrope LLC.

info@digitallycanthrope.com
www.digitallycanthrope.com

Multimedia component of Burmese Refugees, Letters from the Thai-Burma Border can be found at:

www.burmese-refugees.com

Layout Design & Maps by T F Rhoden.
Cover Photo by Khin Maung Kyaw.
Cover Design by Inga Boehm.

inga@waldtraining.de
www.waldtraining.de

Edited by T F Rhoden & T L S Rhoden.

www.tfrhoden.com
www.tlsrhoden.com

Burmese Refugees, Letters from the Thai-Burma Border (2011)
ISBN   0615471072
ISBN-13   978-0615471075

CONTENTS

*Must we really argue that beneficence, trust, creativity, etc.,
enjoyed in the context of a prosperous civil society are better
than the horrors of civil war endured in a steaming jungle
filled with aggressive insects carrying dangerous pathogens?
I don't think so.*

—Sam Harris

I was sitting under the thatched roof of last season's rice crop in the school where I kept my office, when one of the younger students in my English enhancement class brought in a stack of crinkled papers. At first I was not sure what the boy wanted me to do with the yellowing sheets of paper. I quickly remembered that in my exhaustion from leading a full schedule of other classes and discussion groups that morning, I had been too tired to keep up being anything even slightly resembling a proper teacher of the English language that afternoon and had given out a quick assignment to the group of bright-eyed learners to turn into me in an hour.

So here the child was with the class's finished product, well-handled and ink-imbued. I traded a few thank-yous for his disheveled ream of papers and promptly set the pile aside. I knew I would have a chance to look over them the next day since I had nothing planned.

When I did finally tackle the stack, I was very surprised to find the contents within to be captivating and endearing.

The in-class assignment had been something along the following: *Please write three paragraphs about your past.* I had been expecting nothing more than the normal drill of working on the past tenses. But the students' essays to this question ended up being so genuine and their accounts of struggle and disenfranchisement so startling that I knew I wanted to understand better their particular plight.

I wished to learn more about the refugees that I worked with and their unique experiences fleeing to and living in the refugee camps along the Thai-Burma border as well as the complicated process of being resettled to a new host country. When I had another opportunity to meet with the class, I also asked them to write essays about their present situation and future dreams. I did this exercise with most of my classes.

Atop those green-wet mountains that border Thai and Burma, life continued on in the refugee camps as it always had, slowly, sparsely, until my own one-year commitment in the camps came to an end. Given some time to reflect over the experience, I knew it was time to reevaluate those essays to see if they could be brought to larger audience. This book is the final product of that process.

The main objective in compiling this manuscript is to increase awareness about the issues facing refugees and former political prisoners of Burma. Depending on which organization one cites, the total number of refugees in Thailand can vary by the tens of thousands, but most would agree that there are at least 150,000 Burmese refugees living in the camps that border Burma and Thailand. This book will contain accounts from thirty one separate Burmese refugees.

In order for clarity and to help the reader new to the history and geography of this part of the world, the book is broken down into three different sections:

Part I, entitled *8888 Uprising*, is dedicated to what I call the first wave of refugees from Burma. Because of their activities in the summer of 1988, these activists and students make up what is commonly termed the 8/8/88 Generation. They organized what was the largest group of protests since Burma's 1962 socialist revolution.

Part II, entitled *2007 Uprising*, is compiled from stories written by the second main wave of refugees from Burma. These accounts stem from what the international media dubbed the Saffron Revolution in the summer of 2007.

Part II, entitled *Ethnic Strife*, focuses in on the experiences of refugees fleeing from ethnic conflicts or human rights abuses. Unlike in the months and years following the 1988 and 2007 protests, where there was an upsurge in the amount of refugees escaping from all parts of Burma, the dates for when ethnic people fled depends on the particular ethnic group in question and the circumstances of their relationship to the military government.

In compiling the essays, I originally had planned to "fix" the authors' English in these letters. But I realized that too much editing left their work sounding dry and flat. I wanted the reader to hear the voices of the writers of these stories. The only editing I left in was for the sake of adjusting some passages that would have otherwise been unintelligible.

All of the accounts are by the Burmese refugees themselves. All of the writing is theirs. All of the stories are true.

All of the names, dates and specific locations, however, have been altered out of respect for the refugees' right to privacy.

Since some of the narratives are sparse, I have tried to add two or three paragraphs onto the end of every essay to explain the larger situation or to fill in gaps in parts of their story. This mostly involved me writing down my own queries that I had at the time and their answers to them.

I must also mention that in this text I use *Burma* to refer to the country—not *Myanmar*. This is simply because everyone I worked with in the camps called their country Burma (when speaking English). One need not look for a deeper political significance in the issue than that. For this same reason, I uniformly use *Yangon*—not *Rangoon*—to refer to the former capital.

It has been almost a year now since I quit the refugee camps along the Thai-Burma for other projects. I feel honored to finally be able to bring these narratives out to a larger readership.

T F Rhoden
March 2011

From the comfort of my office chair in Southern Germany, I received and read the first of these narratives from my brother. It was, I remember, not as "spectacular" as I had anticipated. Where was the flinty drama of families disabused of their homes, the metallic suspense of nocturnal jungle border crossings, and the icy depravations of life in a refugee camp? It was, contrary to my sensationalist expectations, almost mundane how the narrative showed events leading to this particular refugee-writer leaving Burma and resettling in the camp.

I have come to be ashamed of that initial response in the light of what I now know, have seen, and experienced in the camps. That being said, I am certain that the expectation for the sensational is not too far away from what many readers will expect or hope for in a book like this. We have been fine-tuned to expect as much by our media, and numbed from anything less by information overload.

The awful truths in these individual stories are laid out simply and often modestly. Certainly, the use of English, a universally foreign langue for the writers of these narratives, plays a part, as does a certain cultural restraint. So for some readers it might be easy to find themselves feeling unmoved by what they read here. The flippant way in which so much has been taken from the writers in this collection, and the tenuous circumstances in which they currently find themselves are decidedly not mundane.

As I write this, from the comfort of that same office chair in Southern Germany, it has been almost two weeks since I have returned from interviewing, filming, and visiting with the refugees in the Thai-Burma camps. That one narrative read has led to my commitment in getting these stories organized, presented and disseminated to the widest possible audience.

Our hope is that we have provided enough context and structure so that each narrative can stand just a bit higher than it would on its own, effecting, if not immediate change for the better, than informing and motivating those who can help bring about that change.

T L S Rhoden
May 2011

MAP OF THAI-BURMA BORDER AREA

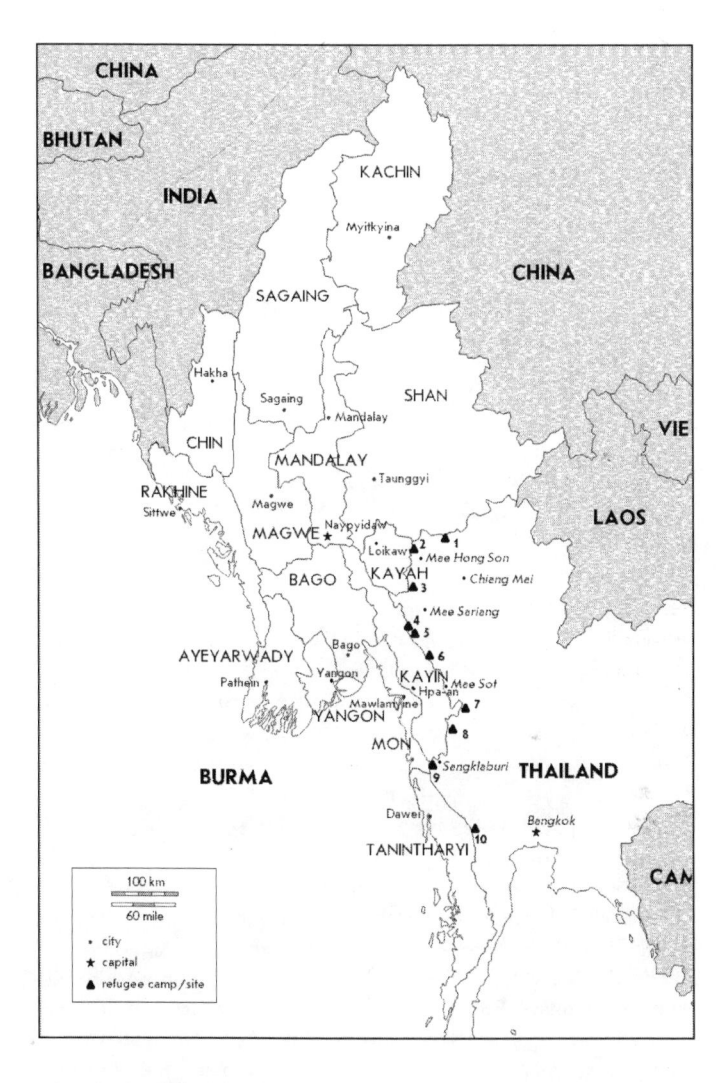

1. Wieng Hang Site
2. Ban Mai Nai Soi Camp
3. Ban Mae Surin Camp
4. Mae La Oon Camp
5. Mae Ra Ma Luang Camp

6. Mae La Camp
7. Umpiem Mai Camp
8. Nupo Camp
9. Ban Don Yang Camp
10. Tham Hin Camp

8888 Uprising

The first wave of refugees that this collection narrates upon date from what is popularly termed the 8888 Uprising and the few following years thereafter. The date August eight, nineteen eighty-eight serves as a useful reference point for any discussion on the everyday individual's struggle for greater liberties in Burma—particularly the right to have some basic form of democratic representation in government.

The nation-state of Burma has had a rough existence ever since official independence from the United Kingdom on January fourth, nineteen forty-eight. The government of Burma was divided politically into various fractions throughout most of the nineteen fifties. Ethnic insurgencies, communist rebels, and even whole regiments of former Nationalist Chinese posed challenges in far-flung corners of the nation for the Yangon-based government for many years (some continuing up to this day). And the Burmese military—no matter what acronym it may have gone under at the time—was never far from the center of administrative power.

However, it was not until the quixotic revolution and following misrule of General Ne Win under his *Burmese Road to Socialism* from 1962 to 1988 that the nation became such a miserable pariah. Blending ideologies of misunderstood Marxism with Theravada Buddhism and Burmese ultra-nationalism (as well as the occasional astrologic superstition), General Ne Win ushered in an era best described as economically incompetent and socially misanthropic. Before the Second World War, the region called Burma was understood to be one of the most resource-rich and economically developed areas of Southeast Asia. By the end of the nineteen eighties this situation had completely flipped, with Burma receiving Least Developed Country status by the United Nations. From every possible economic or social indicator that one could think of, Burma in 1988 could be found amongst the lowest, not just of Southeast Asia, but of the entire world. The nation was rife for social discord and political dissent.

At various times throughout General Ne Win's regime, protests or riots had occurred. But in the spring of 1988 the pro-democracy protests seemed to take on a fresher urgency, whereby the universities were ordered to close. By mid June, in larger cities like Yangon, student protests had become a daily affair. Various pro-democracy groups like the All-Burma Student's Union pushed for having a large-scale demonstration and more inclusive general strike towards the end of summer. August eight, nineteen eighty-eight was chosen for its supposed numerological auspiciousness: the eighth day in the eight month of the year 1988.

The protests continued on for a little over a month: sometimes seeing concessions made on the part of the Burma Socialist Program Party (BSPP, the government's party recognizing that a new election sometime in the future might be worthwhile); other times witnessing horrendous acts of violence committed by the military regime in power. It was during these demonstrations that Aung San Suu Kyi first came into national politics—and to the notice of the international community—when she spoke to a crowd of protesters numbering in the hundreds of thousands in front of Shwedagon Pagoda in downtown Yangon.

On September eighteenth, power changed hands within the military with General Saw Muang taking the central role of head of government. The old constitution was done away with and a new military regime, calling itself the State Law and Order Restoration Council (SLORC), immediately began to suppress the protesters on the streets.

Estimations on the total number of deaths and injured vary

widely on this period, with many individuals still remaining unaccountable for to this day. But across the nation, the general consensus puts the number at about 3,000 who people died during the late-summer demonstrations. Others were thrown into prison. The Assistance Association for Political Prisoners Burma (AAPP) counts that of the 2,073 current political prisoners incarcerated as of March 2011, thirty eight individuals are still from this 8888 generation of activists.

Aung San Suu Kyi's party the National League for Democracy (NLD) was formed shortly after these demonstrations. In 1990, when parliamentary elections were held, the NLD party won 392 seats out of the 429 contested, garnering over eighty percent of the vote. Aung San Suu Kyi's party was never allowed to form a government and she was put under house arrests following the election.

For the two decades that spanned 1988 to 2007, the SLORC was able to effectively maintain a rigid clampdown on the liberties of most of its citizenry. This included the order to not allow Aung San Suu Kyi's party the NLD to form a government, restrictions on travel within the county, the curtailment of a free press, the imprisonment of individuals who were political opposed to the military regime, price controls on many goods, and military-state monopolies on all natural resources (e.g. oil & natural gas, precious metals, timber). Protests did occur occasionally during this period, but they were always something that the military regime could handle. The SLORC also saw successes in dealing with insurgency groups along its borders, brokering numerous ceasefire agreements. However, the only real changes in Burma during this period were mainly cosmetic, as when General Than Shwe took power from General Saw Maung in 1992 and a subsequent name change occurred for the military regime from SLORC to the State Peace and Development Council (SPDC) in 1997.

From a Human Rights perspective the SPDC has been guilty of the following: political imprisonment, torture, forced labor, forced relocations, recruitment of child soldiers, and state-sponsored murder. As this book was being complied, the Assistance Association of Political Prisoners (AAPP) counted 2,189 political prisoners currently incarcerated in Burma. The International Labor Organization (ILO) cites examples of impoverished citizens forced to build military bases, roads and assist in porting goods and military equipment for use in its border insurgent wars. The most recent examples of mass forced relocations was cited by the United Nations (UN) when hundreds of families were ordered to return to disaster areas (regardless if they had homes to return to or not) only days after fleeing from Cyclone Nargis in 2008. The recruitment and use of child soldiers, sometimes as young as ten, in the Burmese army is reported yearly by Amnesty International and Human Rights Watch. The last major cases of state-sponsored murder occurred during the 2007 protests, when plainclothes state agents and other goons were sent out to execute the leaders of this revolt.

As for this section, you will hear the stories of some of the people who took part in those demonstrations, or who were involved with the NLD later on, or who later became political prisoners, or who were family members of those involved in the period following 1988 up to 2007. Letters from refugees who fled after 2007 will be dealt with on the section entitled 2007 Uprising (pg.28).

The Student Party Member

My name is Kyaw Ze Ya. I was a student during the movement of student protests in 1988. I was a university student at that time. The movement happened all over town. I became a member of the student wing of the National League for Democracy (NLD) when they formed a new group on our campus. I was in my finial year at that time as a philosophy student. Because I was in the protests I was arrested. I led a strike to reform parliament with the students in my town. The Military Government unlawfully sentenced me to 14 years of imprisonment in September of that year.

After I was sentenced as a prisoner, I had to live in the prison in Tenasserim Division. We never got normal prisoner rights. I lived in a narrow room that was only eight-by-ten feet. I had to stay in the room all day, except to bathe for thirty minutes a day. The water was putrid and we were only allowed a few buckets to bathe with. All of the food was also not good. It was rotten and the rough rice always contained sand and rocks.

But I understand this is the life of a political prisoner. I don't get normal rights or prisoner's rights. I had to live under the Military Government's orders. After 14 years in the jail, I was released with amnesty in 2002. I was afraid that they would put me in prison again. But thinking of the matter, I am not really afraid of the Military Government, and I will continue to try hard to get democracy and human rights in my country. But for now I must live in this refugee camp.

As I write this an owl is making noises outside of my hut right now on a tree. I hear the sound every night. Sometimes I wake up in my bed, but then go back to sleep. When I wake up I am in a pleasant mood. I pray in my mind that all beings should be happy and secure.

I normally get up about six o'clock. The weather is always raining, but I am happy because I am a free man. In Burma we were never free. Even though here in the refugee camp I have no food for breakfast, and I must borrow from my neighbor's hut, I am happy to be free. I then cook the rice that I borrow and then do any homework that I have.

I find this situation every day. I wonder at what time will this phase of my life be over? But I can't know that, nobody can know that. Why am I in a refugee camp? The only reason is because of the SPDC. I am afraid of them, and their administering and law are very bad for the public. They are always rule with force, and treat the public with force. I can't stand this condition. Because I am political and oppose the military junta, I am a target. So now I live in a refugee camp.

I live in this camp at hut number 630 and I am alone. I had to leave my family alone in Burma. I had to depart secretly; otherwise the government would catch me trying to flee. I am alone now. I don't receive any rations for food yet, because they are still processing my request. I do not understand why it takes many months to process my plea for help?

After I borrow breakfast from my friend, I go to the training centre to learn English. This is wise for my future.

And for my future? What shall it hold? I hope to go to the USA soon.

When I get to America, first of all I want to continue my education. It doesn't matter how difficult the situation is. I will learn everything that is useful for a poor country like Burma. I will do any kind of work that gives my knowledge to improve and undereducated, poor society as I used to live in.

Even though I am old now I want to learn.

When I am a citizen in the US, I have to be careful of the US laws. I will not break the law, and I will take part in maintaining American democracy. I also want to learn how American democracy works and the Western democratic ideal. I believe it is one of the most useful things for Burma.

I will try to find a job that I can apply as much of my knowledge and experience to as possible in the US. By doing so, I can practice my ideas and qualifications directly. If my work involves travelling to somewhere, it would be great.

To be honest, I want to work at a university or college so that I could spend most of my studying. I will share my experiences and knowledge to anyone who needs it. I myself want to use it to develop my country anyway.

Kyaw Ze Ya was one of many who came from this 8888 generation whom I met during various workshops. I remember him being very keen on improving his English, though then again, everyone in the camp who had applied to either the US or Australia was in this boat.

What particularly stood out about him was that he seemed to have an aura of quietude about him—as if he was cautious. He always sat in the back of my sessions and rarely contributed anything unless I directly called him out. But whenever I asked him to speak, he always had insightful stories to add to any political discussion on the situation in Burma. I did not want to pry, but I assumed that his inhibition on some topics were due directly to his struggles, particularly those fourteen years of being in prison for nothing more than having a voice of his own. He was also mum about his activities from 2002 to now, or about how he got into the camps, but that the case for many of the people that I met.

What I liked to see best was when he interacted with the younger generation of political activists who had come over after the 2007 demonstrations. These younger students all looked up to him. Everyone, in fact, from the 2007 protests felt like they owed something to these former students of old who had first stood up against the regime some quarter of a century before.

Since the time that this was written Kyaw Ze Ya has finally obtained an identification number in the camp. This means that he will be able to collect food rations like others in the camps. But he has not been resettled yet. He still lives in the refugee camp alone.

* * *

Hello, my name is Hein Wai Wai. When I was eight years old, my parents moved to a small village located on the Thai-Burmese border. Then I lived with my grandparents to attend school in Yangon, Burma. Every summer holiday I went back home and lived with my parents in the small village. In 1975, I passed my basic education from high school with four distinctions: English, mathematics, physics and chemistry. I got a BS degree in mathematics with qualifications in 1977. Then I also got a MS degree in 1984.

My two great interests in life are teaching and baking. During all my university vacations I volunteered at the state high schools. From 1981 to 1984 I volunteered part time at the Rangoon University Correspondence Department. In 1985 I worked at another university as a part-time tutor and started my own private tutoring service. At that time I looked after my younger brothers and sisters who attended school in Yangon. I have lived independently since I was twenty years old and this contributed significantly to my continuing dedication and hard work ethic which I possess. I value self confidence and hard work. I was very pleased that I give mathematical knowledge to the students—how to think how to solve the mathematical problems in quick and easy ways. I have got good experience in teaching. I have really very enjoyed my teaching life.

By March 1988, students were flooding the streets in protest. On July 23, 1988 Ne Win announced he was stepping down. More violence followed. I also participated in the general strike and I was kicked out of my job. All the universities and schools were closed down for two and a half years, and I lost my job. In 1989 I was willing to serve the National League for Democracy (NLD) party and became a member. I served as general secretary with the NLD at my native township for the 1990 election campaign. Elections in 1990 were won by Aung San Suu Kyi's party (the NLD). But the military junta still ruled the country, wielding absolute power brutally and bizarrely. I fled to Thailand as a refugee when things became dangerous for me a few years later and have been here in the camp ever since.

Presently, my life is very simple. Normally, I go to English language classes Monday to Friday. Every morning I go to the café with my friends. At the weekend, I use the internet at the internet hut. Sometimes, I cook a meal for myself. The meats and food are cheap here in the refugee camp.

The weather is cool, but wet in the jungle mountains. The roads are very muddy and difficult to walk on. Sometimes we slip in the street. It is raining all the time and very difficult to dry wet clothes. The sun does not shine. I often think back to my days in the university system in Burma and miss it.

Since I had to change refugee camps recently I have not got any rations. I am not on the ration food list. I am very upset about the ration system. I am still waiting to learn if they will approve me as a refugee in this new camp or not.

However, the training programs in this camp are great. My current instructors offer to help with a lot of subjects. I am happy about this, but often I am also disappointed and depressed.

For the future, we don't always know what and when something good or bad will happen in our lives. It is also impossible to say that the predictions made by some astrologers are correct. I think it depends on the situation or on each person. So, as a human being I'd like to have a good life as others have.

Once I had many more dreams, and I thought I would a professor all my life. But, unfortunately the situation in Burma forced me to become a refugee. That's why although I hope for the best, I must also prepare for the worst. I won't give up my main aim to resettle to the United States and rebuild my life.

Besides that, one of my first goals for the future would be to find a job. I understand what type of job I can expect to find with my skills and experience. I think learning English will help me to get a better job. However, I would also have to learn English in order to communicate with friends when I arrive in the new community.

It is also important that I must use some time to learn about the United States. There would be some things that I should know about American values, attitudes and behavior that may be different from my own culture. Discovering a new culture is challenging, but it can also be enriching and fulfilling. I hope Americans will welcome me and want to learn about my culture too.

Hein Wai Wai was involved with organizing people to vote during the 1990 elections. Her party, the NLD, eventually won, though were not allowed to take power. She reminded me, if anything, of just your normal modern woman; or, I suppose, that is what she would be if she had grown up in a prosperous civil society. Hein Wai Wai has all the characteristics that would prove successful for any independent, confident woman in America or Western Europe.

Like so many of the Burmese that I met in the camps, what always impressed me was that she was willing to use her inborn talents for something that she believed in, even if it meant standing up against an unforgiving establishment. Like she said, she "value[s] self confidence and hard work."

Most refugees are restricted to the initial camp that they came to. They are not supposed to move around. This is mainly for security purposes. Hein Wai Wai was in an odd situation in that she and around a hundred families were ordered to move to a new refugee camp by the Thai military. The central Thai government wanted to shut down that particular camp. However, in the process of moving these families, a new group of asylum seekers fled across the border. The Thai military eventually decided to keep open that particular camp, even though many people, including Hein Wai Wai, had already been transferred. Unfortunately, Hein Wai Wai's new camp was not properly informed, and she was not recognized immediately as being a refugee in the new camp.

As I compile this, Hein Wai Wai is now on the list of rations for new refugees in this particular camp. There is no indication, however, when and where she might be resettled.

* * *

The Future MBA

My name's Win Maung. After passing matriculation examinations, I joined an institute of technology in Yangon. Sometimes, I feel nostalgic about my university life. I lived in a government sponsored hostel for my hometown which was near Yangon. I met and made friends with many students from various parts of Burma there. Some of my friends were from the highlands of Burma and some were from the coastal areas. Some were from the delta region and some were from the middle planes.

After the first semester, we made an excursion. We went to a little town in the delta region and made camp there. We made fire and played games there. We boy students secretly brought beers. But we didn't know the girl liked hard liquor better.

I and some students became interested in politics in the hostel. In the second year of my university term in 1988, we demonstrated against the military government to call for parliament. Afterwards, we lost our university life because we were arrested and imprisoned for many years. I was enrolled now in a kind of "university of life" in the prisons. Even though I didn't get any degree from this university, I feel that I did the right thing at the right time.

I needed to confront the unfair government at that time!

I arrived in the refugee camp the previous year when the military regime let me out of prison. When I arrived here I tried to accommodate myself to the new surroundings. I encountered some problems. For instance, in my native Rangoon, is hot but the refugee camp is cold, so I have tried to resist this problem. Another problem was water that contains bacteria that can be damaging to the kidneys, so I have had to boil the water to drink every day. The next problem was that I do not have anything special to do, so we were bored. However, I am used to that as a political prisoner.

Now I can adapt to the weather though. I am attending English classes. I don't have any anything else to do here in the refugee camp, so I can focus on learning English. Here in the mountains I wake up at eight or nine in the morning and then go to a teashop to have breakfast. After breakfast I study English until lunch. After lunch I walk around the village for about one hour. And then I take a rest. In the evenings of weekdays, I go to an English training school. After school is done, I have dinner. After that I study more English or read. When the electricity shuts down mandatorily at nine o'clock for our safety, I go to bed. This can be called my formulated life in this camp.

If I have a chance to go to a third country for resettlement, I will grasp it! My dream is to resettle to a nicer country than here. I would like to be a skillful technician. If I arrive to a third country, I will be a hard worker. I will save money in order to go to the university or open a small business. I want to live peacefully.

Most people have a plan or a dream for their future. I am also one of those. In my future plan, there are two main parts. They are education and business. So I'm going to explain my educational plan first.

If I get a refugee number, I will apply to the USA for resettlement. If they will allow me, then I'll fly to the USA. In the USA, I will attend a technical college and finish my degree that I started in Burma before the 1988 demonstrations. At the same time, I will work in a factory or a company as a temp. After I have gotten a certificate, I am going to work for a fulltime job for three years to save money. After that I'm thinking about attending a business university until I get an MBA. That is all for my educational plans

The second plan is my future business plan. If I get an MBA, I'll apply to a company as a manager. If they do not take me, then I will do my own business. I'll run a coffee shop or maybe something else for my own business. But all of my plans depend upon the Thai and USA governments. If they do not allow me to resettle in the USA, all of my plans will have to change. Even though I know that all of my future plans are difficult to implement, I'll try my best. On the other hand, if I never get resettled I may have to spend the rest of my life here in the refugee camp, for I can never go back home unless the politics change.

Win Maung was the most vocal former political prisoner that I met in the camps. Others who have gone through such an experience often seemed much more subdued, but Win Maung was the complete opposite. He also spoke out during sessions or workshops, and whenever I bumped into him along one of the mountain trails, he was always singing some melodic Burmese tune or another.

Like others from the 8888 generation, many of the younger refugees in the camps looked up to him. He could always be found trading stories with them.

I asked him to expound upon his "university of life" idea after I read his first essay. He related it as a way of not feeling sad about not having finished his technical degree at the institute. He said he learnt a lot from other political prisoners, so for him it was type of university.

After the military let him go, he came straight to the Thai-Burma border in hopes of claiming asylum. I asked him if he ever would go back to his native country to which he responded, "only if we have democracy. But I cannot fight for that now. It is for a new generation to fight for it. But my heart will always fight for it."

Win Maung has yet to receive his specific refugee number. Without this number (similar to a social security or national ID number) it is impossible to apply for resettlement in a third country. Unfortunately, it can sometimes take several years before they are allowed by the Thai Ministry of Interior (MOI) to have an interview with the UN to apply for these numbers.

Win Maung still lives in the camps.

* * *

The Brother of a Political Prisoner

My name is Hla Thein. About two years ago I lived in Burma with my family. Although I was poor in Burma I was happy. My occupation was buying and selling agricultural goods. I bought rice, paddy, corn and other goods, then sent them here and there from town to town with my taxi-vehicle. My income was rather good for my family.

One day, in the afternoon, while I had my lunch, my younger brother, who was a former political prisoner, called me by telephone from Mae Sot, Thailand care of my township's exchange telegraph office. The Military intelligence and surveillance were monitoring all calls in from Mae Sot, and they learned about the call. They thought that I had joined the National League for Democracy secretly. I support the NLD, but I have never dared to get involved for fear of being sent to prison like my brother.

At midnight the military officers came to my house, but they couldn't find me because I had gone to my elder brother's house. They continued their look for me night in and night out hotly. My elder daughter posted this news to me. Accordingly, there was now no chance for me to return to my home town. If I returned, I would be caught by them. So I also fled to Mae Sot on the Thai-Burma border. I have lived in this refugee camp ever since.

Later I urged my family to come, but only my two youngest daughters dared to come here. My wife and older daughter decided to stay back in Burma.

My daughters arrived in February 2010. We have lived here for three months. When we first fled to here, they gave us two bars of soap, a mat and a mosquito net. They haven't given us any rations for food yet because we are new people. I hope that they will give us rations sometime soon, because we don't have much money left.

In this refugee camp, my house number is 407 in section 18-B. My daughters are unhappy, but we try to think about resettling to a new country, maybe Western free country. Their names are Sein and Si Si. Sein wants to be a nurse, and Si Si says she doesn't know what she wants to be. Si Si reminds me of my brother who was the political prisoner, so I worry about her often.

Right now I am preparing my hut for the rainy season. This is a UN hut paid for by them. They are providing 25 pieces of bamboo, two logs of wood and 200 leaves thatched together to build our roof. But they are not going to give it to us at all the same time. So far they have only given out 50 leaves for the roof. Next week they will give us another 100 leaves, but I don't know when they will give us the last 50 leaves. I hope soon, for we will have a hole in the roof, but my daughters say that he can cover the hole with some plastic bags.

I am starting to study English, because I must speak English in the USA. But I cannot speak very well. Maybe I can write more than I can speak? Yes, the USA is where I hope to go someday.

I realize that it is not facile to predict our future lives. Because sometimes we get things that we don't need and sometimes we have to be away from what we really need. But I am sure that we are the ones who are waiting for changes that only repeat in on themselves. I don't want to wait for tomorrow to just come. I hate very much waiting for something to change, and so I like to say here in the refugee camp to myself, "Dreams are nothing if you don't work for them!"

We must have future plans and future dreams, but we need not declare them in public. I learned that in Burma and in my business. Never declare to much about anything! We only need to say them to ourselves and measure success for ourselves.

Actually, I have to say that I have a big ambition for my future, but let me not say here what that is. Here in the refugee camp, I am just trying my best to survive and be a good father for my daughters. I feel like I am just at the beginning of my future journey. But, practically speaking, I am motivated to do the best that I can.

Hla Thein was a trader of farm produce and equipment, kind of a middleman in that industry. Hla Thein was adamant that he had never been involved with the NLD, which his brother attested to as well. Of course, it is maddening to think that you could be persecuted for receiving a phone call and have to leave your country. But this is what happened with Hla Thein.

Hla Thein and his daughters, Sein and Si Si, would all three together attend my classes. He wanted his daughters to learn English, though he was more attentive in class than they were.

I felt that Hla Thein' attitude was stoic. His statement, "we only need to...measure success for ourselves," I thought was a good representation of his overall outlook.

I also met Hla Thein's brother, the former political prisoner, once in Mae Sot. He was volunteering at the Assistance Association for Political Prisoners Burma (AAPP), working to collect accurate data on the current number of political prisoners incarcerated in Burma at any one time. Unlike his brother, he was willing to risk being caught by the Thai police for living in Thailand illegally. He refused to live in any of the camps.

Before finishing my work in the camps, I visited Hla Thein's newly constructed bamboo house for some tea. He was still waiting for an identification number.

***

The Medical Specialist

I'm called Daw Aye Aye Shwe, but my nick name is Aye Aye. When I lived in Burma, I started working in government service 1998. At first, I worked in a general hospital in Yangon for about two and a half years. After that, I transferred to a general hospital in the middle of Burma for about five months. As I passed the entrance examination to become a specialist, I came back to the capital city again. I worked in Yangon for five years (including my specialist training). After that I was again transferred to a private hospital, but this time as a specialist.

I had had a problem with the Ministry of Health, Government of Burma in 2004. There is much corruption in the health services of Burma. When I stood up against corruption, my directors said I was a political activist and part of the NLD. This is their excuse and lies. I really just want a better and farer health care in my country. I am not interested in politics, but maybe they cannot be separated? I soon had to flee because they wanted me to stand trial. This I could not accept. My husband agreed to leave with me and the children.

I fled to Thailand in December of 2005. I lived at my friend's house in Mae Sot, Thailand from November 2005 to June of 2006. I enjoyed very much living with my family and his family, but I knew that I was a strain on them economically. I was also afraid of the police since I had no legal permit to stay in Thailand. So I moved to one of the border refugee camps.

At the refugee camp we had to build our own house so there was a lot of discomfort for my family. Later, electricity and twenty-four hour water supply became available so it became more comfortable for us to stay in the camp. Our relatives sent some money to us to buy food and some other necessities. Now we are in the pre-screening process and waiting for an interview with UNHCR and the Royal Thai Government for consideration as refugees.

For the future I know that everyone has an ambition in his life. There is a saying that a person without ambition is like a ship without radar. To fulfill the future ambition depends on how much effort we could make and how strong our desire is.

For me, since my childhood I was interested in machines and instruments. I am also good at drawing. If I could make a choice for my career, I wanted to become an engineer or a computer programmer. But life and education system in Burma is very narrow-minded, so I had to choose something else as a woman. My parents never graduated from university but they supported me as much as they can and want me only to emphasize my studying.

They wanted me to become a doctor like my sister. My relatives from both sides of my parents are not educated, so my parents wanted me to be the envy of my relatives because a doctor in Burma is a good profession. Only if the marks in the matriculated exam are the highest, can one enroll for medical school.

That is why I became a doctor.

At first I was not interested in my future career. But after I had graduated and started to stand on my feet, I realized that I couldn't give up on my career and just do something else. My inner mind likes my career very much. Maybe it is because of the long and difficult years I had to pass through to become a doctor. Anyway, I don't want to quit my job. Later, when I met my husband who is also a doctor I knew that I would always stay in this profession.

Even though I fled to Thailand into this refugee camp, I still have my dreams. I want to be a doctor in the USA. To become a doctor in the US is not an easy and smooth task. I have to study hard for a long time. Furthermore, I have to be patient, hard-working and motivated. I have to take at least three exams and only if I can get high scores in the exams as well as gain clinical skills, can I get the longed-for degree. But I will never give up on my ideas and dreams.

My parents supported to me till I became a doctor in Burma. So I want to return their gratitude by studying hard and getting a MD in the USA. In this way, they will be very happy and proud of my achievement. I am looking forward to reaching this golden day. I hope one day my dreams will come true.

Daw Aye Aye Shwe was a very independent woman. It was not until a few months of working in the camps that I even learnt that she had a husband or children.

The cultural norm that I stumbled upon very early with the Burmese in the camp seemed to be that individuals, when defining themselves, almost always used their relationships with others as their point of personal definition. This often seemed to be even more the case when the person was a woman. For example, most of the middle-aged women I met would introduce themselves as something like the following:

"Hi, my name is so-and-so. My husband's name is so-and-so. He is so-and-so years old. Now he works in so-and-so. My father's name is so-and-so. Come to my house and I will cook you a meal. You can meet my husband."

For Aye Aye though, the first time that I met her was the complete opposite of the norm. After engaging with a score of demur women, similar to the stereotypical example above, I was very happy to find one who could define herself in terms of her own accomplishments (not her husband's).

I asked her once what exactly the corruption was at her hospital. She said that she was tired of having to save medicins and medical supplies specifically for those in the military. She said that she thought that healthcare should not depend on whether one can afford it or if they had the correct ties to the government.

The last time I talked to Aye Aye, she was very happy to announce that she and her family had been put on the list of those to be resettled to the United States. She did not know yet where or when they would depart—most refugees do not get to know their final destination until they look at the boarding passes the day of their flight indicating. She was very hopeful for her new start in life.

* * *

I was born to father Eh Ka Lu and mother Mwe in a little village in the northeast part of Burma. I have four elder sisters and one younger brother. My ethnic group is Karen, not Bamar like the people from Yangon. I was only sixteen years old when the 1988 uprising occurred. Then I joined the National League for Democracy (NLD). When the SPDC took power, two of my sisters fled from Burma and joined the Karen National Union (KNU).

In 1994, I fled to the Thai-Burma border to join opposition groups. I had to secretly go through security checkpoints in our country to get to the border. I lived in an underground news agency, in their office, for about three years [in Thailand]. I had to learn how to use a computer and edit. I also had to study English and the news. I worked as a manager for that office for about three years. I wrote many documents for my Karen language readers.

And then I was sent to the refugee camp by the Thai authorities in 2000. I can still remember that I arrived at the camp at two o'clock in the afternoon. Soon, the camp commander came and ordered us to form a queue in the middle of a rice field. He delivered a speech to us. He then gave us a four-person house to live in.

After I left from Burma, I knew that couldn't go back home. If I went back home I would be arrested. Technically, I cannot live in Thailand legally, so that is why I am here in the refugee camp. I am a country-less person now. The journey to this refugee camp never fails to stir my heart with memories.

Since living here in the camp I have felt in a state of unsatisfied longing. And I am waiting excitedly to have a chance to go to a third country to resettle. Mostly, I would like to go to the USA where my one of my older sisters lives. When I think about my situation, going to a new country will always be better than staying in my home country of no freedoms.

Resettlement is a long and complicated process. Starting over is not easy, but it can be done. I also expect that at first I'll meet some difficulties and may encounter hostility. But in any situation and in any place I'll never be depressed, because both my new husband and I love self-reliance and hard work.

I met my husband in the camp, where we courted and then married in a traditional Karen wedding. My husband is a baker and an expert in making all types of cakes. I am a teacher now in the camp. I have good experience for teaching journalism. With these experiences, I believe that I could also rebuild my life in a third country. And I would like to open a bakery and confectionary or a restaurant where I live. If I have a chance I would like to try to get a PhD degree in journalism if I have time. With my talents, my knowledge, my courage—I'm sure I can succeed.

In the future I will support any pro-democracy movement in Burma and help to make the military regime fall. I will always sacrifice myself and everything that is mine for my beloved country. My greatest wish is to have peaceful movement towards a democratic and federal union of Burma.

I feel hopeful about the future. I hope for success, hope for a genuine change in my country, hope to maybe go home one day. When? I don't know. Let us hope soon and for the best!

She did not mention her name in her essay, so I will call her Ku Wah, a fairly typical Karen name. This is the first example in this book where we have someone from Burma who does not see herself as being part of the main ethnicity of Bamar.

I will talk more fully about all of the different nationals in the last section of this book Ethnic Strife (pg.72), but for now it is enough just to mention that the Bamar ethnicity is typically counted as being over sixty-five percent of the total population of Burma, whilst the Karen make up around seven percent. Most of the Karen reside in Karen State along the eastern border with Thailand (see map).

What I found so interesting about Ku Wah was that she defined her own fight against the military regime as one for democracy first—and one for her specific ethnic group only second. The majority of Karen people that I met in the camp always saw their struggle the other way round: ethnic autonomy first, democracy second.

In the essay she mentions "joining the NLD," but when I asked her what the reach of NLD's presence was in Karen State in 1990, she said that she did not really know. There had been no place for her to "join up" at that time. She explained that as a young adult she just liked the NLD's message, especially compared to her fellow Karens who were more focused on secession than on democracy. Because of her dedication to the principles of representative democracy, I see her as being a better representation of the 8888 generation than of her particular ethnic group.

Ku Wah and her husband were waiting for an interview with the US Department of Homeland Security (DHS) as I neared the end of my time in the camps. When I visited the camps again a year later, I learnt that they had been resettled to New York State.

* * *

2007 Uprising

The second wave of refugees which this book describes originates from the nationwide protests of 2007. By the end of the first decade of 2000, nearly a third of the refugee population living on the Thai-Burma border could be traced back to events surrounding these protests in 2007. The remaining number of refugees mainly came from ongoing ethnic conflicts (pg.72).

For the time spanning the 1988 uprising to the 2007 protests, Burma consistently ranked in the bottom twenty of Least Developed Countries (LDC) by the UN. The leaders of the regime were subject to economic sanctions from the United States of America and the European Union for most of this period. The political, social and economic situation had for the most part stagnated at pre-1988 levels. By 2007, Burma was as ripe at it had been in 1988 for larger scale civil disobedience.

If there is any one point that can be said to have initiated the 2007 protests, it was the unexpected removal of fuel subsidies on 15 August 2007 that really set events in motion. The military regime's oil monopoly doubled the price of petrol and raised the price of natural gas by approximately 500% in one day. Four days later a small group of prominent political dissidents took to the streets to protest the government's incompetence. Though normally dedicated to fighting for increased democratic representation, this small group of dissidents chose to protest specifically the day-to-day issue of economic mismanagement, not the political issue of liberty. Regardless, they were arrested by the government, inciting the condemnation of the US and other Western governments for their immediate release.

On 5 September of that same year some Buddhist monks protested in a similar vein against the military's economic mismanagement, in a smaller township in Magway Division in central Burma. A local military unit broke up the protest violently, leading to one of the first widely reported cases inside Burma where the military had used violence against clergymen of their own state religion. The local monkhood demanded an apology by the military, but it never came. Many monks began to refuse religious service to the military. Planning for larger protests was begun by monks in different monasteries across the country.

A second round of peaceful protests was set for 22 September. Approximately 2,000 monks in Yangon and nearly 10,000 in Mandalay gathered. Word spread and again on 24 September even more of the monkhood took to the streets in protest (purportedly around 50,000 in central district of Yangon). By now the call was no longer for better economic management but actually for regime change at all levels of government.

Simultaneous protests were reported in twenty-five cities nationwide. Most of the monkhood were now completely refusing to offer any of the normal religious services to those in military uniform. A symbolic representation of this was indicated by the monks when they walked through the streets with their alms bowls turned upside down—indicating their refusal to allow military personal to make merit. Bystanders also became involved in various capacities, some cheering, others joining in the protests, others still simply making merit to the monks by providing them with food and drink. These protests held in the last months of summer 2007 were now officially the largest and most organized since the uprising in 1988 a generation before.

By 26 September the military finally decided to crack down on the protests. Troops were sent into the fray primarily with batons and teargas, but many instances of soldiers firing into the crowds of protesting monks were also reported and caught on video. They also attacked the source by entering monasteries and temples across the country to root out dissident monks.

The number of monks injured, killed, or "lost" was estimated to be over a hundred. By the first of October the protests had been quelled, the military was now seen out in full force, and troops were patrolling the streets in major cities.

The international media dubbed the uprising the *Saffron Revolution*, playing off themes of regime change with the Orange Revolution (Ukraine), the Velvet Revolution (Czech), and so on—the color saffron indicating the garb of the monks. In the end though, referring to the uprising of 2007 as a revolution turned out to be a hope more than a reality since no change of government took place.

For this publication, the majority of narratives will be from individuals both who were directly and indirectly involved in the protests. Many of these people may not have even taken part in street demonstrations, yet with the months of military clampdown following the uprising, many were later accused of playing a part in the lead up to or execution thereof.

The Film Student

I am Yin Yin Aung. In 1990, I was born in Myanmar, also called Burma, which has been ruled by a group of military officers, an oligarchy. However, I grew up in one of the villages in Burma up to grade ten. At that time, I didn't know how other countries in Southeast Asia have developed and how universities and students have improved outside of my country. This is because all of us students had no right to learn what we need to know. As you know, the military regime controlled everything for students and the public.

As a student, when I lived in Burma, I regularly wanted to go to university to learn what I wanted. I wanted to study cinematography.

Because of the monk protesting in 2007, we, all the students gathered to demand for our freedom and democracy. We wanted to help the monks. At that time, Burma's military crushed protesters by the tens of thousands of monks, students, and other citizens, who had marched in anger over the rising fuel prices and decades of repression.

After taking part in protests in Yangon, Burma's military officers interrogated and arrested many demonstrators to put in jail for many years. Because I was involved in the organization of other students to help the monks, the military police were searching for me. I would never get fair trial. So, I think that there is no point in staying in Burma. Therefore, I decided to go to a refugee camp on the Thai-Burma boarder, to settle in another country—like a democratically elected government, and join the university or college in this country for a more beautiful future.

When I first arrived in this camp, I admit that everything was very difficult for me. And I often felt really bored after the excitement of the 2007 protests. Maybe also because I don't have a job. But now I am a student again in the camp for the English language. My schedule is now repeated over and over again every day.

Now I am learning English because I desire to go to America. I like learning English, but I hope that my instructor would change my nickname. He calls me Neon, but I don't know why. When I hear that, I feel really scared and I imagine a dead body in my mind because I saw that once in Burma under the neon light during the monk's protests. A student friend died under the neon light above and his skin look like a dead man's skin. I hate that memory.

However, now I feel good to live in this camp. I have a lot of new friends. Sometimes, I visit the waterfalls and streams in the mountains near the refugee camp with my friends. This makes me feel happiness and relaxed. Sometimes these places make me remember my native land and all of my old friends. I am satisfied to live in this camp and I like my instructor's teaching methods. I feel I can learn a lot before I am resettled.

Now that I have an official asylum at this refugee camp in Thailand, and I am waiting for my turn when the UN gives me the chance to settle down in the USA. So the most important question is, what would my future career in America be.

I'm really interested in cinematography. My dream since I was young is to be a very talented movie director who always creates monumental works in the film industry. Now the time is coming to make my dream come true. So as soon as I get to the USA, I'll join the New York Film Academy. And I must try to express my latent talent in art to be an outstanding student.

To be a successful film director one has to face a lot of challenges like in the creation of art, advancing technology of filming devices, visual storytelling, criticisms and so on. I understand that it is not an easy job. Film directors always have to use their effective ideas from their hearts. So I want to say the work of a film director uses not only their brains but also their hearts to engage movie audiences.

Being a successful film director means having a chance to give messages about my own feelings and also about others to the movie audiences. I can also entertain the people with my beautiful work that comes out from my soul and heart. If the audiences are satisfied with my work, I will be o proud of myself. That's why I have decided to try hard single-mindedly to be a successful film director as my future when I resettle in America. I would like to do a film someday about our struggle in Burma.

Yin Yin Aung was involved in the student wing of protests in 2007. I was curious about how much involvement the students had in planning these protests, since they seemed to have stemmed mostly from the monks' initiative. She said that, unlike the 1988 protests where the students were the primary mover, the students were taken as unaware as the rest of the population when the monks first moved out onto the streets. The students who ended up joining the protests simply saw this as an opportunity and jumped at the chance to air grievances that had been fomenting for many years.

As the time of this writing, Yin Yin Aung has, unfortunately, not been granted an interview with the US Department of Homeland Security (DHS) yet. Due to the number of refugees, this process can take as long as a year or two before a refugee is granted an interview for asylum to the US. Once granted though, and a refugee is accepted for resettlement to the US, the process normally takes another two to three months before the refugee actually sets foot on an airplane to their new life. Where that new location in America might be is normally not disclosed until the refugee has the boarding pass in their hand.

* * *

The Unemployable Physicist

My name is San Tha Aung. I lived with my family at a village in Rakhine State of Burma. There were five members in my family. They were my parents, younger sister, my younger brother and me. I finished middle school at my village. I came to the town alone after that and I joined high school. After I passed 10th Standard [high school graduation], I went to the university in the capital city of my state in Burma.

My specialization was in physics. There are eighteen townships in Rakhine State, so many students were from different places in the state. We met at the university in Sittwe. Sittwe is the capital city in Rakhine State.

At first I was really happy in the university when I joined it. All the students regularly attended university for three years. Unfortunately, the military junta does not help to support us in school with scholarships, so we have to pay our own way. We were happy when we got our degrees. Yet there were no jobs for us after that. Because the military junta's family and their closely connected friends control the good jobs everywhere in Burma, it is impossible to find a good job without that nepotism. Even if you want to work for the military government, you must give a lot of money to buy your job. Therefore, I tried to find a job in a foreign country, but I was not allowed a passport. You must also pay a corruption fee for a passport in Burma too.

In September 2007 the revolution of monks started. This was when I ran into a big problem. When I unexpectedly saw a monk and two protesting men with wounds on their heads, I took them to a clinic. Even though I'm not Buddhist—I'm Muslim—I still felt like I should help them after they were beaten by the soldiers.

However, the soldiers saw me and followed me home. They were going to arrest me, but I ran from the house and escaped. Some policemen and junta thugs were after me after that. I had to decide what to do next, but in the end after talking to my family, my father said I should flee from Burma into Thailand.

After I escaped Rakhine State in the west of Burma, I was afraid when traveling to the Thai border in the east of Burma. But I made it here safely. I am now staying in this restricted area as a refugee. I live in section 13 of the refugee camp.

I have been staying in this camp since 2007 then. All the refugees in this camp come from Burma. There are various ethnicities in this camp. The camp is situated in the mountains along the Thai-Burma border. We are currently supported by the Thai Burma Border Commission (TBBC) for our food rations. I am lucky, because not all refugees get rations. I also get my medical from Aide Médicale Internationale (AMI). I am very thankful for that help.

I try not to think about my father and mother in Rakhine State, because then I become very sad. I feel sometimes like I have abandoned them.

Winter is the coldest season in the camp. I don't like it because the hut cannot block out the cold mountain air. I like the summer season. But in the winter season, we make various competitions with the sport NGOs. There are a lot of fun games and sports and I am happy then.

Now, I am trying to resettle to another country for my future, but I don't know which country I will resettle to. I hope that some Western government understands our situation. If I return to Burma I will be persecuted unfairly.

I am happy now in the refugee camp, but I always miss my parents and my younger brother and sister.

Everybody should have a specific aim for their future. For different people there are different ideas about their future. They may have more or less objectives in the future and for their practical lives, but we should have exact goals for our future. This is what I believe.

Honestly though, I have no idea what my career might be in America. I know that I want to study physics again when I resettle, but I worry that that may only be a dream. I hope to go to America, but I know that everyone hopes to go to America in the camps.

America would be different. Indeed, the culture of a super-power country is totally different from Burma's. We are from an undeveloped country. We have a great lack of knowledge, ideas and even language skills for using English.

For the time being, moreover, America has a big economic crisis at the moment. I think this is also a great barrier to getting a job easily in America. And for a refugee, I feel that I have poor preparation for a future career. Though I have learnt some vocational skills in the refugee camp like how to fix an engine. It is like physics, but on a smaller level.

Apart from this situation, I do not feel depressed about the idea of my future, whether it is in America or not. At the moment, I am working at a school here in the refugee camp. So, I have to deal with volunteer teachers and am responsible for working with persons and staff from nongovernmental organizations. Out of these people, some are native speakers of English. Almost every day I speak and work with English-speaking teachers. At the same time, I am also a student in their classes. So I dare say that my language skills have been improving gradually. I can learn their Western culture, their ideas and other valuable knowledge. It is a priceless experience for me.

Maybe the education field for me in the future would be appropriate? I hope so, for I feel not equipped to do a factory job, even if I can now fix an engine. But I can do that type of job if it necessary for my survival in the future.

San Tha Aung was one of the least political people that I met in the camps. Though he complained about the military regime like everyone else did, he seemed more concentrated on the practical issues of just finding a job. He did not mention it in his essay, but the military regime in Burma does discriminate against Muslims, particularly those from Rakhine State (pg.78). Oddly, many of the Burmese that I met thought of Islam more as an ethnicity than a religion. He mentioned that he was unemployable because he could not afford the price needed to bribe his potential employers, but I imagine that there may have been discrimination issues as well.

At first I assumed that San Tha Aung must have been more involved in the protests than he initially wrote, but he swore that he had only wanted to help one monk who looked like he might die of hemorrhaging.

I inquired if he had had the opportunity to contact his parents since coming to the Thai-Burma border. Thankfully, he is able to contact them about once a week by phone. He told me that his father is saving up money in order to bribe a local official in their hometown to not arrest San Tha Aung if he comes back.

He is currently deciding whether or not he should return home or apply for resettlement to another country.

* * *

When I was a child, I liked to go to the swimming pool. I used to swim after school with my friends and sometimes we went fishing on the weekends. We enjoyed cooking fish at home with my family. I spent most of my free time near that stream in my hometown. My full name is Maung Maung Tin, but my friends just call me Maung Maung.

I grew up gradually and became a high school student. I always hung out with two pretty girls. But finally, these girls broke my heart and faded away from my life. Maybe because I try for both, they both stopped liking me. After that experience, I decided to concentrate on my studies. I tried my best with my studies and passed the matriculation exam with good marks. I chose to go to the Institute of Technology in Yangon to study computer programming.

While I was learning at the university the monk uprising happened. I wanted to support the monks. They are our leaders for morality, so when they say that something is not moral like the government, it is probably true, I think.

I participated in the strike as a good student, because I also disagreed with many of the government's policies. The regime caught many of my friends at that time and they were after me as well. I helped to plan protests, so I knew they wanted to catch me too. I didn't dare to live any longer in my homeland, even if it meant that I could not finish my studies.

I fled to the border line of Burma and Thailand after that.

Now I have been here for about one year and six months. In this refugee camp there are some bad points and some good points for me to think about. There is often nothing special to do here so I am often bored. There is also no electricity and the water contains too much lime and calcium, so it is not good to drink. However, for good points there is an English training school and also there is a computer internet hut on the Thai side outside of the camp. These are good for me.

I normally wake up at eight or nine and then I go to the teashop to have my breakfast. Then I go to learn English. To be honest, English is very difficult and sometime very boring. Nevertheless, I have to learn English because there are no higher-level books written about computers in my own language. They are all written in English, and I want to be a computer programmer. I would like to go to the US some day and work for them. But that is only a dream I feel?

In the evening after dinner I take a walk on the outside of the refugee camp, but sometimes we are not allowed from the security regulations. I miss having more freedom even though it was not a very good freedom in Burma. I drink some coffee in the evening to relax. I like coffee very much, but I can't drink too much in the refugee camp, because the water is not safe here. My hut has no electricity so I must always go to bed when the sun comes down.

I have some dreams about my future while I live in the refugee camp. The first dream is that if I arrive to a third country. I will work any job to save money. When I have enough money to attend a college or university, I will attend it. I am interested in technology and something in the computer field. So I will study technology and computer subjects at the college or university. I will study it to get a degree.

My other dream is to save money and open an internet shop. Before I open the internet shop, I will learn about networking between computers, because I want to connect the computers together well and block against viruses. Another reason for opening the shop is just because I enjoy using computers and the internet, so I want to open an internet shop.

If I win a big lottery in the third country, I will visit China to behold the Great Wall. I will also visit throughout Europe. And I will go to England to watch the Premier League. I am therefore interested in football. And I am a fan of Manchester United Club. I will buy a mansion and an expensive car after I graduate from college.

But to have such a bright future I must first leave the camp.

Maung Maung Tin was able to get a job whilst living in the refugee camps at the satellite phone and internet hut a few

kilometers from the camp. A refugee having a job is rare. The Thai military discourages such things. From their perspective, if someone is going cross their border illegally and claim asylum, then they should not also expect to have the right to take jobs away from the Thais. Maung Maung's job though was not at a wage that any normal Thai would take. He said his Thai employer paid fifty Baht a day for his work. He took in twenty Baht a day, while the other thirty Baht was given over to the Thai guard at the gate as a bribe to allow him to leave the camp area. He seemed happy with the arrangement.

On the days that he did not work, he would visit my English enhancement classes. Most of his questions in class though had to do with computers, of which I know very little. From someone somewhere he had gotten hold of a ratty old copy of a C++ college textbook for computers. He would always carry it around with him in his sling tote bag.

I asked him how he had been involved in the protests and he said that he and a best friend were very active in trying to release information onto the web during that time. Doing so was difficult though, since the military shut down all the servers in the country—something that they do quite regularly.

Maung Maung is currently waiting to be called in for a resettlement interview with the Australian government.

* * *

The School Committee Member

I lived in Rakhine State in Burma. My name is Zaw Win. I passed 10th Standard in my home state. After I had passed the 10th Standard, I moved to Yangon to study medicine at the university there for about a year. But I couldn't study that anymore because I needed a lot of money. So I said to my parents that I would study another subject.

My parents permitted me to learn another subject, whatever I chose, so I studied about law. While I was studying, I had a conflict with one teacher from the university. We had different points of view in politics. This is not allowed in Burma. That teacher was from the military junta. He said I must agree with him or I would have trouble and not graduate. I said that I didn't like that process.

When the monks started their uprising, I decided to join them. I believed that what they were doing was the correct decision for our country. The teacher who was in the military saw me and reported me. I soon found out from colleagues that I going to be arrested. Burma became dangerous for me after that. I had to make a decision to stand for an unfair trial or flee. I choose to flee.

I have now been in Thailand for two years. But I only arrived in this camp nine months ago. I always miss my own country.

Now I am a committee member at the local English training centre. I like studying English and learning more about it.

This refugee camp is in Thailand along the border with Burma. There are fifteen different parts to this refugee camp. The scene of the camp is actually very beautiful because it is located in the mountains. However, the weather is bad for me. The rainy season is very heavy and the winter is very cold. Our clothes do not dry easily in the rainy season because of the heavy rain. It is also difficult to sleep though the whole night during the hard winter.

Unfortunately, we also have to walk a long distance to get drinking water during the summer when the mountains become dry. However, the refugee camp is safer for me than staying in a town like Mae Sot where we are illegal aliens.

Sometimes there are skirmishes between the Karen

National Liberation Army (KNLA) and the SPDC near the refugee camp. I hate the fighting and the sound of gunfire. Sometimes, I am really afraid when I hear that sound. But the fighting hasn't reached the camp yet, so that is good.

All in all I feel lucky because some NGOs come to help us. Aide Médicale Internationale (AMI), the American Refugee Committee (ARC) and the UN assist us in some areas. For that I am thankful. But I always miss my homeland.

I hope I will get permission to leave the refugee camp later this year in November, because for three days in November in Mae Sot and Myawady there will be a celebration for the full moon. I think that I will be very happy during the full moon festival. But if the Thai military does not allow me to leave the camp for that time, I will celebrate here in the camp instead. I know that I will celebrate the happy New Year festival in the refugee camp.

I hope that in April, the USA government program Department of Homeland Security (DHS) will interview us. After that if I pass the clearance interview, I will have the opportunity to leave the camp forever. I will go to the USA. I hope my future will be beautiful in the USA. My aim is to get married, study law, and someday become a famous human rights lawyer in America.

Zaw Win was very active in helping to run activities at the local English training centre. He only mentioned it briefly here in his essay, but that is where her spent most of his time in the camp. Since I kept an office at the same centre, I got to know him and the other committee members of the school very well. He was always planning some activity or searching for some outside funds to keep the centre going. It was through this same teaching centre that I met all the people who have contributed to this publication.

I liked working with Zaw Win in particular because he always had stories to tell about what it was like living in Burma under the military regime. He had a way of making these stories seem very tangible for someone who grew up thinking of democracy as a given in my life.

He was set up for an interview with the DHS, but this was pushed back. This is quite common. There is no way for a refugee to accurately gauge when a meeting with one of these organizations might be kept or broken. A typical refugee is completely at the behest of four or five large bureaucracies (e.g. UNHCR, Thai government and Thai military, DHS for the US government or some other third-country government, and so on). If any one of them changes a scheduled meeting or simply makes a clerical error in one of the refugee's paperwork, then they can expect to wait even longer. The challenge of coordinating between so many mammoth-sized bureaucracies is one of the main reasons why it can take so many asylum seekers more than five years before they are resettled to a third country

* * *

I am U Zaw Gyi. I was born in Yangon. I graduated from high school from my township in 1991. And then I graduated with a BA from my university in 1998. Firstly, I worked for a logistics company in Burma until 2001. We sold imported foods, stationary and household liquids. My owner was a Singaporean.

I then went to work for another company. This company did business internationally. We also accepted foreign currency, did some foreign exchange and used international credit cards, so I met a lot of foreigners. Unfortunately, our company had to close down when military government increased taxes. We also did not have enough to pay for their bribes.

Then I went to work for a jewelry company until 2007. We sold various kinds of jewels with precious and semi-precious stones. Some were made out of good silver and 18k gold. All of the jewelry was cut with modern cutting machines. My owner at that time was Burmese. We accepted foreign currency and credit cards, so I again met a lot of foreigners. I envied the freedoms they enjoyed.

I enjoyed this profession and working for corporations, and thought that I would do it for a long time, but then the September 2007 protests happened. I wanted freedom for my people, so I protested against the military junta also. I dared to go out onto the streets of Yangon with my fellow country-men. I was fired because of my involvement in the protests.

I had to escape from Burma in the end of 2007, when the country became unsafe for me. The military was going from house to house trying to find people that participated in the protests. I did not want to leave Yangon, but I had to in the end.

I now live here in this refugee camp. I stay with another family and my house is near the English instruction centre. I usually go to the centre on foot to improve my English. I know that English is important for international business. Even some Chinese use English now. My teacher is a good teacher. He teaches us new vocabulary, and modern American usages and slang. This is important for getting a normal job in America.

The weather is very cool every day, but sometimes it rains too much. The climate is the wettest in July and August. Our refugee huts and trees shake by the strong wind. In this camp, the market is just okay; I miss a real market, like what we had in downtown Yangon. The refugee camp's market is only open on Mondays, Wednesdays and Fridays very early in the morning. On the weekend, many people go to church or some people go to the Buddhist monastery.

All in all, I guess that like this camp. It is safer for me than in Burma. Though, I miss having a normal job and normal life. The camp is situated between hills and mountains. It is in an attractive forest with many bamboo trees. Every refugee makes their hut out of bamboo, and also the roads and their chairs and tables. Bamboo is used for everything. It is a beautiful place to look at. Even though I miss the city I am happy that I escaped to here.

I hope that I will be permitted to go to the United States of America within the first half of 2011. All of us try to make plans like this, but I really hope to go.

A journey to the USA by plane will be very long, so I think that I will be very exhausted. After landing in American and with four to five days of rest, I will start to attend ESL classes in my new city. Then I will look around the town and near-by areas to learn the area. I will try to observe my new country's habits and cultures.

I will study and memorize the streets of my new town, which will help me to get a driving license. I will try to take the United State's driving license examination after knowing the main streets and countryside and their driving rules. After that, I will apply to get some credit cards and give back my debt for the air ticket gradually. We have to pay back our air ticket that the US government paid for us. I will try to get a job before the sponsored money is cut off, so that I can give back.

By doing a part-time job, I think I will have a chance to learn the American way of doing business. I want to visit many states of the USA for my own business some day. One year after arriving in the USA, I will be ready to apply for a Green Card. After receiving the Green Card, I would like to visit Thailand to look for an opportunity to do business between Thailand and the United States. In a few years my life will have much more happiness than usual.

U Zaw Gyi's story was very inspiring for me. He essentially had a stable middle-class life in Burma: corporate job, private apartment in Yangon, motorbike, and enough money to send back to his parents. That he was willing to gamble it all on joining the 2007 protests is a testament to a very strong character. Since I have had some experience in the corporate world myself, I could not help comparing myself to U Zaw Gyi: would I have been bold enough to join the protests like he did if our situations were reversed? I can say that U Zaw Gyi would make a perfect candidate for a corporate governance position in the West. Though, knowing him, I think he would prefer to work in sales.

He mentioned in the essay that he wanted to pay his plane ticket back once getting on his feet in the US. This is true: refugees to America are required to pay back the fare of their tickets. Most do, slowly, a little bit every month.

As can be imagined, in times of economic depression in an industrialized nation, refugee resettlement programs like these are often some of the first things to be cut from a government's budget. That a refugee is required to pay back assistance like airfare and other things helps arm politicians with reasons to argue for the continuation of such programs, since the recipients will be required to pay back the assistance.

* * *

I was born in the Bago, Burma (the ancient capital of my country) and passed my high school examination in 1997. Later I moved to a township in another division and there I worked farming mushrooms. I disliked being a farmer, so I thought about entering the monastery. After some time I took the rights to become a monk. I enjoyed learning about the ways of Buddha.

In 2006 I started to attend a Buddhist seminary for further study. However, my studies soon had to stop. In the meantime in 2007 there was a surge in petrol in my township in Magwe Division and spread to most of the prominent cities of Burma. I personally supported the monk's practicing of *pattanikkujjana*, meaning the monks have the duty to remind the government when they are diverted from compassion and justice in their ruling system.

On 22 September 2007, I joined in and marched with about two hundred monks in the streets of our township, chanting Buddhist religious verses to make our request known by the government. After this there was a crackdown on the religious lives of monks.

Therefore, I had to flee from my house in the end of September 2007. During three months from that time, I felt my situation unsecure and moved to another village. Then I contacted the student affairs at the Buddhist seminary and was told that I had been dismissed from school and that if I came back, they were ordered to inform the authorities. After that I had to move again. It was not safe now to be a monk, so sometimes I wore plainclothes for protection.

I understood that I would not be safe living like this, and so I travelled to border region in January 2008 and arrived in Mae Sot, Thailand. That was a hard trip through the mountains and checkpoints to Thailand. I always worried that someone would learn that I was a monk who had protested.

I later learned that there were many other Burmese refugees living in camps, so I left Mae Sot and arrived to the camp in February 2009.

I now live in the monastery in the refugee camp. I am now studying English at this training course; it is my favorite subject. I think English is an international language in the world and so it is essential for me.

I don't like living here in the refugee camp, but I am a refugee, therefore the camp is the only place to go for political asylum for me. I must live here. The weather is very wet, cold, foggy and always raining here. My robes always have mold. I don't like the rain so much. However, I can't complain about the food too much, because I can eat fresh vegetables grown in the jungle. So I like that.

I always remember my parents and all my friends and I want to see them, but I cannot go there, back to Burma, because I am a refugee. I don't want to go back to Burma until it becomes a free Burma with democracy, because I am afraid of prison.

However, I have decided to make my life the best I can in the camp. I still chant every morning and evening in the camp monastery, and I try to read scripture. It can calm me. I do not want to resettle. Even though I am afraid to return to Burma, I do not want to go to the West. I must therefore wait until the situation is better in my home country.

My future is in Burma. I shall return to my homeland when it is safer for me again. I am resolute about my return home some day.

He did not mention his name in the short letter above, so I will call the monk Aung Aung Shwe. I heard many stories like his in the camps from other monks. Most of the monks like Aung Aung Shwe were participants more than ringleaders in these events, but all of them had passion and all of them were committed to regime change.

Aung Aung Shwe used the word pattanikkujjana *in his description of events and as something of a duty for the monkhood at that time.* Pattanikkujjana *is a Pali word used by Buddhist monks to indicate a refusal to accept morning alms from those said to have violated religious principles. Refusing members of the military the opportunity to make merit in this way is one of the clearest signals that the monkhood can send that they are dissatisfied with one policy or another. The last time that a large majority of the monkhood practiced pattanikkujjana against the military regime was in 1990 when Aung San Suu Kyi's party the National League for Democracy was not allowed to form a government after winning eighty percent of the national vote.*

Aung Aung Shwe was also one of the only few people that I met that did not wish to be resettled to a third country. I wondered if he was worried about the refugee camp shutting down some day or about the Thai military sending him back over the border. He was not worried though and said that he would wait it out. He was convinced that as long as the current regime remained in power, there would always be refugee camps like this along the border. And if the government did change or become truly democratic, then that would be his signal to return to Burma.

* * *

The Video Gamer

I am Lay Byu. I was born and bred in a state in the northwest of Burma. My family had a small farm, and I had to help them with farming. But sometimes when I was in childhood, I used to play video games without knowing of my parents. After I played video game, I got corporal punishment. I had a lot of best friends. They were really good. Whenever I got in trouble, they helped me out. By the way, I was born on August 8th 1992.

When I was in grade 8 at high school, I saw a girl. She was really good-looking. She was in the same grade with me, so I made her a friend of mine. We were very much best friends, but I knew I loved her also. So I asked her to please love me too. She said yes. After that I was the happiest boy in the world. But this didn't last too long because the military junta wanted to arrest my father for helping Aung San Suu Kyi. We had to flee into Thailand to this temporary refugee camp.

When I was in Burma, I was really happy. There were a lot of my relatives, my friends, my teachers, my high school and my girlfriend. I sometimes used to hang out with my friends, if I got some free time. I miss all of them, especially my girlfriend. Occasionally, I pray for going back to my native town.

Many people who come from Burma have moved to neighboring countries, especially Thailand in order to flee oppression. We must now struggle for our survival. Fortunately, we have gotten refugee status and we live in different camps. Maybe you can understand why we must become refugees? It is not easy.

I have been in this camp for two years with my family. Before this I lived in another refugee camp farther away. I have known many other refugees who are now my friends and they had various cases and political and economic reasons for leaving. Some left for ethnic reasons. Due to our government we all lost our rights, but we are lucky now to escape and be refugees. We now have chances for education.

On a normal day I always wake up at 7 o'clock with the chickens and then listen to radio from 7:10 until 8 o'clock. My job is then to feed my pigs no matter if it is rainy or shiny. My father makes me do this job. After I feed my pigs I take a bath and go to the school at 10:10. I am trying hard to learn English day by day. I am at the intermediate level of English.

Before now I never read any books, but I have changed my mind in the last three months because our foreign instructor has encouraged us. Now I listen to the radio and read books. I think that I can get a better pronunciation if I listen to Voice of America (VOA) in English. I know that my English is not the most perfect, so I am trying to be more confident. I hope to use English when I resettle. This is my life right now.

My father says life will be better in the future. If we resettle I can study for the GED and then go to a university.

Lay Byu like many younger students took part in workshops or classes in the camp. What I found most interesting about many of them was how much they reminded me of all the other teenagers in the world—how much they reminded me of myself when I was younger. Despite living under a military dictatorship, political repression, strained economic conditions, and limited educational opportunities, kids will be kids the world over. That Lay Byu was more interested in writing about young love or how he would try to skirt his chores at home to play video games should serve as a reminder that we are not all that different.

Lay Byu was not involved in the 2007 uprising. He would have been fifteen at the time and he said that his father did not allow him out of the house at that time. However, his father was involved in the protests and a member of the National League for Democracy (NLD), Aung San Suu Kyi's party.

* * *

The Activist's Daughter

My name's Cho Cho Aye. In the past I lived in a township outside of Yangon, Burma. I started to attend school when I was six years old in my childhood. I was happy in school life. But I had a misfortune in grade seven because my mother was arrested by the government. She was a political activist for democracy in Burma. After that I had to live as a motherless child with my father. I lost my mother's platonic love. My father was also arrested twice, when I was in grade two and grade four. I got my high school diploma in 2003.

I attended English classes at the NLD office in Yangon. In my leisure time I taught my neighborhood's children. I loved them and they loved me. By teaching them, I learned a few words of the Karen language and about their culture. I later fell in love with a man who was a political prisoner who also worked at the office.

I liked to volunteer at the American Center Library (ACL) too. I met a lot of knowledgeable people. I had a chance to attend English language programs and I passed the intermediate class. I also volunteered at the Moon Shade Kawina Association (MSKA) by counseling people living with HIV/AIDs (PLHA) with my senior co-workers. I used to take a bus to go to my school or other places where I wanted to go. I would also go to the hospital to for counseling PLHA. At the first time I could not stand the smell of the hospital. I loved to work in charity because I lot of experiences.

I attended university in Yangon and my major was mathematics. I didn't finish my university degree because we had to flee from Burma. This was because my whole family was too involved in politics. All of us are NLD party members. After the 2007 monk protests, it was not safe to stay in Yangon anymore.

I only attended university through to the second year, but I do have a high school diploma. I am not satisfied about this in my life. I want to finish school. I will have to try and go on in my life.

My life in the refugee camp now is very simple. I usually wake up at six o'clock, but sometimes at seven-thirty. I normally have breakfast at eight and then I brush my teeth and wash my face. Sometimes, I have to cook a meal for my family, but I am very lazy to cook a meal, because I don't want to get up on those mornings. In the camp, I often feel less motivated than I did in Yangon. But I must try. I always must try for everything—that is a refugee life.

My older brother gives duties for everyone in my family: one person has to cook a meal three times a week, and we divide that duty up. I always enjoy myself when I go out with my friends. Thankfully, my boyfriend fled with us, so he is here. We will be married soon in the camp. For this I feel blessed

I always go to school at eight-thirty, because my house is too far from the school. When I finish my English lesson here, I have some training classes I can attend. Every weekend, I usually like to go hiking in the mountains near the camp with my boyfriend. I want to be healthy all the time. However, I always miss my home country

Compared to my past I imagine a simple future, so my future might not make you feel exciting. If I get the chance, I will go to a third country and will resettle there. I'll go back to university to finish my degree. I might even learn another language. I will find a part-time job for my expenses. I won't waste my time in my new country, because I have to try and struggle for my goals.

If I had not come to this refugee camp I could probably go back to my home country. Sometimes I want to go back to my country. But I think it isn't possible for me and my future husband or my family anymore. If I could go back to my country, I would join the teacher's college. I would probably found a preschool. I love children and I want to be a founder of an after-school program.

But now I am planning for resettlement. In order to stay with my boyfriend we will be married before we apply for resettlement. I hope for a bright future!

Cho Cho Aye was incredibly active in the refugee camp. She mentioned that sometimes she feels lazy in the camp, but I

never saw any proof of this. She was always volunteering her time or lending a hand. Whenever a NGO came into the camp, she was always first to welcome them and offer them assistance with anything they might need. I often saw her walking around with some visiting UN official or another, offering herself as a translator or guide for the camp of 15,000 people. When she said that she used to volunteer her time with all of those organizations in Yangon, I believe it.

She did not mention it but her mother was released from prison after five years. During the instances that her father was in prison as well, Cho Cho Aye's grandmother would look after her and her siblings. They all live together now in one hut in the refugee camp.

Normally, a family like hers, when resettling, would be processed as one unit by the UN and other refugee agencies. When a youth is over twenty, they have the choice to be processed with the family unit or alone. In order for her to be processed with her boyfriend though, she needs to be married. Since there are no civil law offices to register a marriage in the refugee camp, this normally entails requesting the Thai military commander of the camp to attend the ceremony and sign a prepared document stating that he has witnessed their wedding ceremony. Cho Cho Aye and her fiance are currently planning their wedding ceremony.

The Conscience-Stricken Pedestrian

I lived with my family in a village in Chin State of Burma. There were four members in my family. They were my parents, younger sister and me. My name is Shwe Saw Win. My father was a farmer and my mother stayed at home to raise us. The first time I left my village was to study high school in the town.

After I passed 10th Standard, I went to the main university in Chin State. My specialization was literature and the Burmese language. I only attended university for two years, because my father's field and home were occupied by the Military Junta. There is always a tension between the Chin farmers and the government. They just took our land. So my father was jobless and then they expelled my family from the village. He had to leave and go somewhere. In that time, we had some friends who helped us for the absolute necessities in the capital city of Chin State in Hakha.

This man helped my father and our family. He allowed us to live in his garden in the city. We are trying to look for a new job, but I found one for the family. I had to drop my education from the university and started to work at an ice factory. My job was to send ice all over the capital.

However, after working for one month in my job, the September Revolution of monks started in 2007. On that day I saw a monk when I was walking home from my job wounded by four or five thugs. I didn't want to leave the monk to die, so I took him to the hospital. This was a mistake. Some policemen and others were after me after that. It was not safe for me to stay with my family anymore, so I had to flee my town and my family stealthily to Thailand.

Now I live in this refugee camp.

These days in the camp I'm trying to focus on the future. If I have the freedom of movement, my future career in a third country (maybe America?) will be a life that is better than here in the refugee camp. If I would arrive in the US, I would take additional English classes the first thing I do.

I think I am lucky because I have relatives on my mother's side that live in New Jersey. Not all of us refugees have such relatives, so I feel blessed about this. They have a factory which produces new clothes. I would like to work part-time with them.

There are some NGO and volunteer organizations that I want to support when I resettle. I will try to become a volunteer and undergo intensive training in the ERI (Earth Rights International) office, which is in the US. This organization is involved in the environment and human rights issues in Burma. I like this group because they want to help my country.

I want to finish my university degree, but I know that I cannot study Burmese language in the West. That is okay. Maybe I can study something more useful for making money to send back to my parents. I accept this now.

If you ask me was it worth it to help a monk on the street, I must answer I don't know. Did you know? I am not a Buddhist. I am a Christian. Many Chin are Christian. But I think I would help the monk again if I had to live the situation again.

But maybe now I have a better future if I can go to live with my relatives in New Jersey?

Shwe Saw Win was very proud of his home state and ethnicity in the west of Burma bordering on India: Chin. He was always quick to say that the majority Bamar ethnicity looked down on his people. In fact, I learnt very quickly that even in the refugee camps tensions existed between many of the different ethnic groups. Even though they had all fled from Burma for safety reasons, they normally divided themselves within the camp so that there seemed to be a Karen area of the camp, a Bamar area of the camp, a Chin area of the camp and so on.

I asked if there were other reasons why he might have fled, not just that he was seen helping a protesting monk. He said that his family had always had problems with the local government and that there was one local military officer in particular that wanted to have another reason to trap his family. He did not want to describe more than that, aside from adding that one should never try to do business with the military government. He said that if there is a business disagreement with the government there is no legal recourse.

At the time of writing Shwe Saw Win was scheduled to have an interview with DHS. Having relatives in America can often help to sped up the process. In general, it is easier to set a refugee up in America if they already have family there waiting for them.

* * *

When I was younger I was a student. In the eighth grade I was doing high school in my hometown. However, there was a student revolution in 1988 against the military government, and I participated. They shut down the univer-sity for some years after that so I could not attend. Because I protested with my fellow students they would not allow me to attend upper education. Instead I went into business for myself.

I had a movie rental store. I rented and sold cassette tapes, video tapes, CDs, MP3s, VCD, and DVDs. I gave my rental store an English name for good marketing. I called it John's Video, because my English nickname is John. I did this for my livelihood for many years and it was okay. I also became interested in recording and helped a local music group make audio recordings. But it wasn't enough to support my family after the fuel prices were raised in 2007. In my country we did not have enough money after that.

I protested again against the military junta in 2007, like as I did when I was still a high school student in 1988. This time the government wanted to arrest me. I knew I could not keep my family here anymore. We had to flee Burma after that for our safety, and then we made it to this refugee camp.

This is why I live in this camp now.

For my future I don't want to have a boring job for my whole life. I mean I like to work for a job that I am interested in. In the future I will probably not have a video store anymore. I have so many other positions that I might like to take. If I have to select one for my future, I would choose to work for some music production companies. I would like to work as a sound-audio engineer.

Actually, it is my dream. If I would take such a job, I have to get a degree or diploma in sound-audio engineering first. I know that such opportunities are in America, so that is where I would like to resettle with my family.

Before I could take that job, I would have to work many part-time jobs to get some tuition money for such an education. I want to create the best mixes for the singers and customers. I don't know exactly that my future desired job is the best or not. But I know that I would be very happy to work with the music. After I have gotten a lot of experience from small recording companies, I can surely apply for a popular music production company. Maybe this is a dream, but dreams are good, no?

If I have some money to develop my own music production company, I would do my best to become the well-known music production company. And I am sure so many popular singers would like to make contracts for their albums with my music company. I don't want to work under someone else, so I'm sure I'll try my best to run a company with my experience and saving money.

So, I know that before I go to America, I must learn English well. If I can speak or understand English well, I can attend a sound-audio engineering school easily and can pass job interviews. That's my desired job, but if it doesn't come true then I will try something else. I know I must work hard for my living in America.

My family is depending on me. But I know I need a degree at least. And I have to continue my studying in America to get a higher position.

Will I ever go back to Burma with my family? My answer is only if we have the appropriate freedoms.

Unlike many of the other refugees in this collection, who only participated in either the 1988 uprising or the 2007 uprising, John was involved in both. He said that he was never a leader in either protest, but that we had been eager to join in. He told me that he felt lucky that he was not arrested in 1988 like many people that he knew. He was mainly able to avoid detention because he was still only a middle school student at the time of his first demonstration.

In 2007, when the monks began their protests, he again joined in the demonstrations. What may have been a fad in youth—protesting against authority in 1988—was, twenty years, later a true grievance. The government's mis-management of fuel hikes had a direct effect upon John's livelihood. John said that he was very eager to take to the streets when he saw the monks demonstrate.

After the crackdown that followed the 2007 uprising, John's neighbors reported to the police that he had taken part in the protests. Fortunately, when he decided to flee with his family, he said that he was able to sell off his inventory of DVDs and VCDs quickly—enough money to make it to the border of Thailand and begin the process of resettlement.

* * *

The Travel Agent

I was born in near the capital city of Burma. My name is Maung Maun Lwin. I studied primary level, middle and high school level from 1978 to 1991. I passed high school level in 1991, but I could not go to university cause during that time our country's political situation was not too quiet. Our university was closed from 1990 till 1993.

In 1993, our university opened so I went there to study. I learned in our science university in Yangon. My major subject was chemistry. I studied there about four years and I got a bachelors of science in 1997.

After that I was looking for a job. Fortunately in 1997 I got a job in a travel agency. My post was a van driver. So I travelled a lot of the tourists around my country.

I was a workaholic, so in 2002 my boss changed my job to tour operator. I was happy about the news, but in 2007 the Saffron Revolution started by monks happened in my country. I decided to walk around the city and protest with the monks. I and my family went to this refugee camp when we had to flee for our safety for being in the political protests. We came to this Refugee camp in 2009.

I have been staying in the refugee camp with my wife for three months. We don't get food rations from TBBC yet. This is because it takes a long time before they will accept us as real refugees. My wife's aunt, three brothers and one sister also live here in this camp. They do have rations, because they have been here longer.

I have been learning English in this centre and also with some other instructors. I am also learning Thai to better communicate with locals. There is a Basic Business Training here in the refugee camp and I want to join that as well. In my free time I work for the student newspaper of our English centre. Sometimes, I join the training of agriculture when they have sessions. I like to keep busy.

The refugee camp's weather is very rainy now. In the winter it becomes very cold. I don't like the camp's weather. This camp is very dangerous to walk around in the rainy season, because the roads are not good. I often slip and curse. But I always go to my classes and training.

We will get more information in March 2010, but after

that I plan to apply for the USA resettlement program. I want to have a chance to settle in the USA with my family. I will like to stay in California, because my brothers stay in there. I hope they can help my family. When we arrive to the USA at least four months will be for leaning basic English.

I graduated from university with a BS in Chemistry. Now I am interested in tourism management, so I will study in a California college. When I graduate from a California college with a degree in tourism management, I can apply for a job at a travel agency or a ticket call center. I will make an application, sending in my CV and a cover letter, explaining why I want a job.

When I get a job at a travel agency, I will learn through in-house training courses within the company. I will try to be a pro-active person in the company. I want to work at least three years in the company because I want to promote our country's tourism business.

I hope I will get a lot of challenges, because most Americans don't know about Burma and our culture. So first I will advertise that Burma has a lot of historical places and recreation places. I hope at that time our country's policies and politics will be better. I hope many Americans will come and visit our country.

Maung Maung Lwin was very guarded about his past, which is understandable. He did not want to say much about his involvement in the 2007 protests aside from mentioning that he did protest.

The times that I talked to him outside of class or bumped into him in one of the camps many huts that had been turned into a teashop, he was always very eager to talk about places to visit in Burma. It was evident that he had been an enthusiastic travel agent in the past.

He stated that he was not getting food rations from the Thailand Burma Border Commission (TBBC) yet. Since many of the camps are so porous, with locals often coming and going at will, it can be a challenge to recognize who is truly a refugee and who is not. TBBC does family headcounts, going from hut to hut in each of the camps a few times a year. It is important for a refugee and his family to be present at their hut when this census is being tallied. Otherwise, one may be left off the list. It is therefore not so uncommon to be in a position like Maung Maung Lwin, when you have arrived in the camp claiming asylum, but have come either too early or too late for the TBBC count.

Since writing this description, Maung Maung Lwin has now been added to the TBBC ration list.

* * *

My name's Thien Thien Lwin. I was born in 1989 and I grew up in a township outside of Yangon. I wanted to be a businesswoman. When I was ten or eleven years old, I used to do a small business, which was selling betel nut and snacks. I enjoyed selling it because I can meet people and get pocket money from that. In my childhood, I also used to ride my bicycle with my family around my town. I was very happy and I had a best friend who name was Khin Ma Gyi. She had a lovely smile and was very kind to me.

When I was a teenage, I had a lovely boyfriend. My happy days were when I went to a picnic with my friends and boyfriend in Yangon. Firstly, we arrived at one of the restaurants. At there, Khin Ma Gyi had ice-cream and cake, and me and my boyfriend had a coffee shake and bread for lunch. And then we continued to the traditional area of the city. This was very nice to see. I was very happy because I visited this old part of town with my boyfriend and Khin Ma Gyi.

Back then I wanted to learn how to swim, but I couldn't swim. So my father taught me to swim. When I could swim, my boyfriend and I went to the swimming pool. I used to be bad at swimming, but I am better now.

I was a good cook in my family. So I invited my boyfriend to my house and I introduced him to my family. After that we had our enjoyable lunch.

Last year we got married, but then we had to come had to this refugee camp when my uncle and his family were persecuted for being involved in politics.

I have been here now in this refugee camp since 2009. When I arrived here I was surprised because I had never heard about a place like this before I came. Many different people with different habits, cultures and religions are here. Everyone is more accepting than in Burma. However, at firsts I was very fed up with this place, because it is not very safe or clean. I am always thinking how I could have come here. But after some time I became more happy and decided to do my best and stay.

Now as I have been staying here for a while, I have become very happy, more than in Burma. One day I decided to join a camp training school. I started to learn at a food and bakery course. At the course I learned many kinds of Thai foods and now I feel confident to cook many types of cakes and cookies and baked items. Now I have finished the course.

This year my husband and I have gotten our numbers for resettlement to a new country. That is why I am studying English now, so that I will not face hardships in my new country. I will be happy in a new, third country. I am trying very hard every day.

In the future, I have never learned about the economy, so being a business woman will be difficult for me. But now I will study about business. I want to be a wealthy person in my future. I will attend business classes and I will get a certificate on that. I will try my best in business to be self-organized and self-motivated and also computer literate. I can meet very well-known people in the world in business.

I should gain more experience and get a degree for my career. I will invest my money in China and also in Burma. I want my country's business to be the top in the world.

I can use my income to help children and people who live with HIV/AIDs if I have the chance to do that. After I am a rich person in my life, I also want to be a NGO founder. I want to help orphans and uneducated people. My native country is very poor in education, living standards and essential needs. I love children and they are the future of our country. When they study more they can create more in their own style.

Before everything though, I have to study to improve my life. I'll have my friends and family. I shouldn't lose touch with my instructors and friends.

Thien Thien Lwin and her husband were both cheery. They would attend my intermediate level English class together. I never saw them far apart from each other.

They were very well liked and respected in their camp. Though neither of them had been involved in either the 2007 uprising or politics in general—they both admitted to never protesting directly—their simply being related to people in the National League for Democracy (NLD) party made living in Burma dangerous for them.

I did not quite understand this until I witnessed other refugees' reactions to them. Whenever Thien Thien Lwin mentioned her uncle or other members of family, the listener would always be taken aback. They were considered to be stars in their camp. Thien Thien Lwin's uncle was well known for being an outspoken NLD party member and very much respected. This same reverence had passed down to Thien Thien Lwin in the camps.

I was curious if everyone in Burma who was related to someone in the political opposition was in the same situation as Thien Thien Lwin and her husband. She said that there is a culture of turning in one's neighbors if involved in politics, but that most of the time the local government cannot be bothered to do anything about it. The majority of such cases seem to be random disagreements between two individuals, where one side irrelevantly accuses the other of being involved in politics to win the local military over to their side.

However, in Thien Thien Lwin's case with her uncle, he obviously posed enough of a threat to the government that the military felt it pertinent to also keep tabs on his next of kin. She said that that is not normal for all politically connected families.

In the description she mentioned receiving her "numbers for resettlement to a third country." What she meant by that was that her husband and her had gotten their refugee identification numbers from the Thai Ministry of Interior (MOI). She had not received anything yet that would indicate that she will resettle though. Thien Thien Lwin and her husband are currently applying for asylum in the West.

* * *

The Assistant Clerk

I am Myin Soe. When I was in kindergarten I had two lovely friends. One was a boy the other was a girl. We loved one another; we understood one another. We helped one another when we needed help. We went to school together, and we played together. When we had holidays we went to the cinema and the zoo with our parents. At that time we were very happy. I never thought one day I would be living in a refugee camp.

When we passed 10th Standard, one of my friends had to move to another place with her parents. I also had to go to Yangon. I could say that our togetherness and happy-days faded away after that. When I was in Yangon I soon looked for a job. At first I had some difficulty in finding a job but later I got a job and I felt very happy because of the work I could now do. But one day, something evil happened.

One day when I was on my way to work, I saw a lot of people who were on the road demonstrating. Some of these people were just monks. I saw them when they were beaten and arrested by soldiers. Some were running and shouting. I saw a soldier kill a monk. I was very afraid to see that kind of scene.

On that day I went back home early because that event kept coming back to me and I could not work. When I came back home, I felt sick. Even though after two days I could recover again, I can't get that event, with the monk killed by the soldier, out from my memory.

I never thought about being a refugee before I came here. Why would I? Would you? But I now know that life can be a struggle. I try not to complain and instead pray to Buddha to help me in the difficult times. I am sure that I will have to live in this awful place for a while, so I pray often. No man can avoid or run away from all that is bad or unlucky in life, so we must face this even though we don't know the future.

I am flexible, so I don't mind too much about the present situation. But I do miss my past time and my motherland. Now I have been staying here in this refugee camp for five months and one year. I don't want to count my days here, but I can't stop it. My daily life in the camp is very simple. I work as an assistant clerk in the refugee high school on weekdays.

I play basketball with the children in the evening but not so often. I am also doing an English enhancement class with our foreign instructor. He is friendly and kind-hearted. I'm proud of being one of his pupils.

However, I am getting fed up with some of the unusual people here, the muddy streets, the unclean water, the harsh environment and so on. Sometimes, I think my dreams are gradually fading away and away. So I am active in trying to engage with the UNHCR, but the refugee process is very slow. I do not understand why. But I don't care, because I know that I will never return to Burma

Rereading many of the essays here in this compilation, I was struck by how many of the people have resolved to make the best of the situation as they can. Many of the writers seem to possess an amazing capacity for hope. Initially, I did not know where to place this letter in relation to the others, because it did not seem to fit. But after reviewing the particular case of Myin Soe, I knew that it would be an injustice to leave this essay out for simply for editing reasons.

The small amount I knew of Myin Soe is the same small amount that the person reading this book knows about him. I do not know why Myin Soe fled to the camps. He never told me. I respected his not wanting to talk. All I ever learnt about him was what he wrote in this English language assignment. I think though that for what he left out in terms of events, dates and other descriptions, he made up for in honest emotion.

It is important to remember that many other asylum seekers like Myin Soe in the camps feel just the way that he does: angry, fed up, even hopeless.

* * *

The Politician's Son

My name is Khin Zwar Win. I would like to tell you about my past. I reached this refugee camp in 2009. My father was a politician. It is not safe to be a politician who is opposing the government. He had to run from the Burma military when they put out an arrest warrant for him. He fled here and lived here in the refugee camp for four years. Now he lives in the USA after being resettled.

In 2000, I left from my hometown and moved to the town with the Three Pagoda Pass, which is on the Thai and Burmese border across from Sangkhlaburi, Thailand. I met my wife there and I married her. In 2006 we had one daughter. Her name is Kin Shet Lin. I love her very much and miss her now that I am away from her. This is because I missed my father very much and wanted to make contact with him. So I crossed into Thailand and met him in the refugee camp.

At that time, before I left I asked my wife if I could see my parents and she agreed. In 2009 I made contact with my father. After many years he got really lucky because he was sent to the USA. He told me, "Don't go back to Burma. There is no future there. You must follow me." I agreed with him, so I haven't left the refugee camp. I am trying to convince my wife to cross over to the refugee camp to, but it is a very difficult trip. She is afraid to come. I miss my family very much.

Someday I would like to be an education organizer. I want to support my native country in education. Most poor people cannot expect to attend their appropriate level of study because they cannot afford to pay for the student tuition. I am really upset about our educational system. It is a dog-eat-dog society in Burma for many children. In my hometown, children cannot attend their school, because they have to try to get food by selling vegetables, newspapers, ice water, or doing work as housekeepers. There is no time or money for school.

The government is very strict about a political person's children like me. They restrict their movement and do not allow them to attend school. They threaten the teachers or tutors or professors into not allowing my children to study. Even when they have passed the matriculation exam, they are not allowed to attend the university.

For the future I want the education to be fairer. Right now we have no hope. We are living without a future because we do not have proper education and technical learning for our society.

Khin Zwar Win was not the first person that I met in the camps who had left behind family. It is not uncommon for a person who has fled to go many years without seeing brothers, sisters, parents or even a spouse or child.

As this was being written, Khin Zwar Win said that his wife was still nervous about making the move to Thailand. Three Pagodas Pass, where they lived in Burma, is a famous crossing point through the mountains that border Burma and Thailand. Moving across from the Burmese side to Sangkhlaburi on the Thai side would be relatively easy. What Khin Zwar Win's wife was wary of was the trip from Sangkhlaburi to the refugee camp high into the mountains, more than a few hundred kilometers away.

Since Thailand is neither a signature to the 1951 nor 1967 United Nations Conventions Relating to Status of Refugees, the country is not required to recognize asylum seekers if it chooses not to. This was the case during the nineteen seventies, when the majority of refugees fleeing into Thailand at that time were either from Cambodia or Laos, and this is the case today with Burma.

In both instances, because of international pressure (and a simple unpreparedness for the sudden influx of refugees), the Thai government and military were forced to relent and carve out temporary safe havens for these people on their territory. However, at no time is the status of refugees in Thailand, whether housed in the camps or making their way to the camps, considered to be legal under Thai law. Because of this situation, if Khin Zwar Win's wife and child were caught by the police without proper identification they could be arrested.

It would then be up to the local police whether they chose to ship them to one of the refugee camps or deport them back to Burma.

Khin Zwar Win said that because his father was a renowned politician in the NLD party, he would sometimes be harassed at the government high school. He did not graduate high school and said that the main reason he left his township for Three Pagodas Pass was to go to a place where people did not know he was the son of a dissident politician. Once in the camps though, his situation mirrored Thien Thien Lwin's (pg.64) in that whenever he mentioned his father's name fellow refugees were quick to praise his father's work.

Khin Zwar Win is still waiting for his wife and child to follow him.

* * *

Ethnic Strife

The last section of this book concentrates on refugees who have fled from Burma because of ethnic strife. Unlike the first two sections, no specific dates or events serve as unifying turning points as to why these people have sought asylum across international boundaries. The dates and events of each group's struggle depends upon the specific relationship between that ethnic group or sub-group and the Burmese government. Each ethnic group has a unique history with the military junta.

For practical purposes, the Burmese government has grouped all of the multifarious sociolinguistic groups in Burma into eight "major national races." These are Bamar (also Burman), Shan, Kayin (also Karen), Kayah (also Karenni or Red Karen), Rakhine (also Arakanese), Chin, Kachin (also Jingpo), and Mon. Bamar is the dominate sociolinguistic group in Burma with nearly 70% of the fifty or so million people that make up that nation-state. The Shan make up approximately 9% and Kayin around 7%. The other major ethnic groups account for less than the remaining 12%, but it is exceedingly difficult to find accurate numbers on any of these groups. Since the last census taken by the military junta was in 1983, international and government agencies like the UN, World Bank, CIA have all had to come up with their own estimates, each conflicting slightly with each other. In fact, the last major census that anyone in the international community trusts comes from the 1931 population census performed by the British colonialists.

Within these eight national groupings, the Burmese government recognizes an additional 135 distinct ethnic groups. However, there are also a few other groups that the government refuses to recognize for political reasons. Modern-day anthropologists of Burma put this number even higher. One challenge when discussing these ethnic groups is deciding which name they ought to go by. Because of the ruler-resistance dichotomy between the government and many of these groups, the term the military regime uses is often not the name that the particular group call themselves. In deciding which names to use with each ethnic group, I have decided to go with the name that I encountered the most in the camps when speaking to a representative of that group. For example, all the Kayin people I met called themselves Karen and the majority of the Rakhine (also spelt Rakhaing) people I knew referred to themselves as Arakanese.

In this book, six major ethnic groups will be discussed. They are Karen, Shan, Mon, Chin and Arakanese. Kayah and Kachin are not represented here, since none ever attended my classes. Bamar, the eight group, is represented throughout most of the narratives from the 8888 and 2007 Uprising chapters.

The Karen

Approximately three and a half million people in Burma and along the Thai border can be classified as Karen. The majority of these people live in Karen State (also called Kayin State). They also make up the majority of refugees living in camps along the Thai-Burma border.

The Karen were promised independent autonomy by the British if they were to side with the Allies in World War Two, which the Karen did. When it came time for negotiations with the British for independence, Karen leaders were, however, left out of the process. In 1947, most of the Karen boycotted the general election leading up to independence, a move that further left them out of the process for taking a part in the consti-tutional assemble. In response to these events, the Karen National Union (KNU) was formed later that year. After colonial independence, the KNU's first demand to the newly formed government in 1948 was independence from the Yangon-based government. The new Karen country was to be called Kawthoolei with roughly the same borders of modern-day Karen State.

By 1949, the situation in and around Karen State became violent when the Karen National Defense Organization (KNDO), the military wing of KNU, began to wage war against the central government. Both sides, officially, blame the other for the start of violence. Fighting was sporadic though consistent through the nineteen fifties and sixties. The KNDO later evolved into the Karen National Liberation Army (KNLA) and was at its strongest during the nineteen eighties, when they were said to have had an army of over 20,000 volunteers according to a KNLA retired general of that time. These days, because of fractional divisions, that number has dwindled considerably. Much of their military funding is purported to have come from black-market activities, primarily smuggling.

This war between the KNLA and Burmese military has been ongoing since 1949. Aid agencies estimate that there are currently at least 200,000 civilians in and around Karen State that have either had to flee higher up into the mountains of Burma for safety or cross over into Thailand. The rate of Karen refugees fleeing into Thailand stems directly from this fighting.

In this section of the book, four people will give their own accounts of the situation.

The Shan

There are estimated to be approximately six million people in Burma and along the borders with China, Laos and Thailand that can be classi-fied as Shan. The majority lives in Shan State but can also be found in Karen and Kachin State.

Unlike the Karen, the Shan were

included in the negotiations that led up to indepen-dence in 1948, specifically the 1947 Panglong Conferences in Shan State. They were able to effectively argue for regional autonomy and a unique opt-out clause in the 1947 constitution after ten years if the newly created union with the central government did not prosper.

Even with these agreements tensions between the Yangon government and the Shan leaders were never far from the surface. However, the catalyst for open calls of a completely independent Shan state did not occur until General Ne Win's socialist revolution in 1962. The opt-out clause was not honored by the central government and the formation of the Shan State Army (SSA) occurred afterwards.

Fighting between the SSA and the military junta has been going on intermittently for the past forty years. During this time the SSA has split into Northern and Southern factions, and other ethnically Shan-based armies have also emerged to join the fight like the Eastern Shan State Army, also known as the Myanmar National Democratic Alliance Army (MNDAA). Alliances between these ethnic armies are always tenuous and are constantly in a state of flux.

Similar to the Karen, the number of refugees from this conflict rises and falls with the tides of battle between different factions of the SSA and the military government. One striking difference though between Shan and Karen refugees is the Thai government's complete refusal to recognize any Shan people fleeing from fighting as refugees. There are a few reasons for this, but the most cited are the SSA's close relationship to narcotics production and trafficking in the past, the Shan's shared sociolinguistic ties with the Thais, and the inability to distinguish Shan migrant labor with Shan asylum seekers. In order for a Shan person to gain entrance to one of the border camps, they often have to claim a different ethnicity.

In this compellation, there are two accounts written from the perspective of Shan people. One is the story of a woman involved directly in the fighting as part of the SSA, whilst the other account is written from a civilian's perspective.

The Mon

There are estimated to be between one to two million people in Burma that are of the Mon ethnicity, though some agencies count more. The majority can be found in and around Mon

State, which shares a small stretch of border with Sangkhlaburi, Thailand around the area known as the Three Pagodas Pass.

During talks for Burmese independence from Britain in 1947, the Mon also sought self-determination. They were largely ignored by all the other parties concerned. When a revolt broke out in 1948, it was quickly put down by the newly independent Burmese government. Mon separatists moved into the mountains, regrouped, and organized themselves as the Mon Peoples Front (MNP), later changing their name to the New Mon State Party (NMSP) in reaction to General Ne Win's revolution. The armed wing of their organization goes by the name of Mon National Liberation Army (MNLA).

Unlike the KNLA and the SSA of the Karen and Shan, the Mon's fighting force has been less well funded. The most lucrative source of income that the MNLF have found has been trade along the Three Pagodas Pass. This has led to continued fighting with not only the Burmese military but with the Karen to the north as well.

The greatest concession made to the Mon by the central government was the creation of Mon State in 1974, though this proved to be more of just a name change than any additional autonomy. Since 1995 there has been a cease-fire agreement between the military government and the MNLA. Occasionally, fire fights do break out between the Burmese military and the rebel army, and whenever they do the conflicts invariably create new Mon refugees.

This book contains two different accounts of refugees from Mon state. Both stories are told from the perspective of villagers living near or in the war zone.

The Chin

Chin is a catchall word meant to include many different ethnic subgroups like Laimi/Chin, Mizo, Kuki, Zomi, and others. Approximately a million people belong to this Chin grouping, the majority in and around Chin State or across the western border in Mizoram, India (see map).

Representatives of the Chin people were invited to the Panglang Conferences in Shan State before independence from Britain, though unlike the Shan who gained the right to form a state as part of the new union, the Chin homeland was instead broken up into divisions. Not until much later in 1974 were the Chin allowed a state in the union.

Compared to other ethnic groups mentioned here, the Chin were never as well organized. Because of this, human right abuses (e.g. forced labor, torture, extra-judicial killings) committed against the Chin were largely unknown to most of the international community until within the past two decades.

In response to the 8888 Uprising (pg.6) leaders in the Chin community formed their own party, the Chin National Front (CNF), along with their own paramilitary wing, the Chin National Army (CNA). Unlike the rebel armies that belong to the Karen, Shan and Mon, the CNA is sorely underfunded and consists of less than a few hundred volunteers.

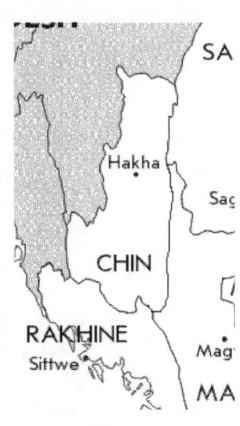

Most of the Chin refugees therefore do not flee from war zones, but from human rights abuses. Many others are forced from their lands to make way for military nationalization projects. Another point of tension between the central government has always been that the Chin do not adhere to the state religion, Buddhism. Over eighty percent of the Chin are Christian. Chin State is also considered the poorest region in an already impoverished nation. The UN estimates that over forty percent of the population is not getting enough food to survive.

When the Chin do flee for human rights abuses, they do not have the luxury of jumping the border to Thailand, like the Karen, Shan or Mon. Instead they must make an 800 kilometer journey before they even reach the border of Thailand. Some flee across the border into India, but since there is no international presence of aid agencies there, most are simply forced to return to Burma either directly by the Indian government or indirectly due to economic reasons.

In this book two stories are provide from people of the Chin ethnicity. They both account cases of human rights abuses by the military junta.

Approximately three million people belong to the Arakanese ethnicity, which like the Chin is a term including many smaller subgroups. Most Arakanese can be found in and around Rakhine State on the west coast of Burma and along the borderline with Bangladesh and India (see map). The majority of Arakanese are Buddhist, but because nearly a quarter of them follow Islam, Rakhine State has the largest Muslim population of any region in Burma.

Similar to the Chin, no Arakanese representatives were invited to the 1947 Panglang Conference in Shan State. The Arakanese received a state in 1974 at the same time as the Chin. But like the Chin, this proved to be nothing more than a name change for the region.

Politically, the Arakanese response has been fractured ever since colonial independence with many groups claiming to represent the region's interests such as the Arakan National Liberation Party (ANLP), the Arakan Communist Party (ACP), the Arakan Independence Organization (AIO), the Arakan Liberation Party (ALP), the Arakan League for Democracy (ALD), the Tribal National Party (TNP), and many more. The least fractured military group is the Arakanese Army (AA), but their size is as small as the Chin National Army.

Similar to the Chin, the main exodus of Arakanese refugees from Burma into Thailand stems from human rights abuses. All of the same charges that have been levied against the central government for the Chin have also been applied to the case of the Arakanese.

In this collection there are three stories from the Arakanese ethnicity. The first two appear in the 8888 and 2007 Uprising chapters of this book (pg.6 & 28), whilst the third is found in this section.

The Farmer

I am called Shi Mon. I was born in a small village in Karen State in 1981. I started my basic education in that small village. After I passed my basic education, I moved to Hpa-an, the state capital, to continue my education. I passed high school in 1998, but did not do very well. Therefore, I came back to my village and worked in the farm until I came to this camp.

When I was young my mom died. I am the one and only son, so my father loved me very much. But one day when I was four or five years old, my dad and I went to my aunt's village. After that he left me with his sister and never came back again. So I don't know if he is still alive or dead. My aunt took good care of me like her own son all the rest of her life.

Here is some important parts that I would like to tell you.

In our village, all the villagers were farmers. They grow rice in the paddies and many kinds of plants. When the SPDC troops came into our village we had to run and hide in the jungle. If you did not, then they would catch you and torture or kill you. Sometimes we had to carry their loads and equipment from place to place as a porter as forced labor. If they did not see anybody in the village they took everything they want. Sometimes they burned down the whole village just because they can.

Shi Mon did not stay long in the refugee camps. When he attended my sessions, he was always very lively and eager to participate—so much so that when he was not present, I noticed his absence quickly. After two or three weeks of lessons missed, I asked some others in the class where he had gone. I was relatively new to the camps at that time, so I just assumed that he had been resettled and was waiting to hear the

good news from some of his classmates. This, however, was not the case. He had instead gone back into Burma.

Out of all of the ethnicities that I met in the refugee camps, the Karen were the most likely to return to their homeland. Within the Karen community, news travels quickly about battles between the KNLA and Burmese military and about which spots along the border are "safe" and which are not. This means that a sizeable proportion of the Karen do have the opportunity of returning to Burma if they tire of the refugee resettlement process—which can last many years. This does not mean that they can return to their home villages, since those are often destroyed, but they can return to a place currently under administrative control of the Karen National Union (KNU).

This short essay is the only record I have of Shi Mon's life in Burma. Other classmates later confirmed that he had gone back across the border and returned to Karen State. They said that he had joined the Karen National Liberation Army (KNLA).

* * *

The Youth Pastor

My name is Ning Kee. Timmy, my English name, was chosen by myself. I was born on May 12, 1981 in a township in the northern part of Chin State. I grew up from a Christian family. My parents are Rev. Thang Guang and Mang Tun. There are nine of us in my family.

In 1987, we moved to another township. My father served as the president of local bible college. In 2003 I started to study at a Christian college in a township very near Yangon and I graduated in 2007. In the year I finished also a bachelor of arts in psychology from a state university on the east side of Yangon. After graduating I was appointed as the youth pastor of our church back in my hometown in Chin State.

I married in 2008 and have a daughter. As the youth pastor I visited and preached in the villages around my town.

One day while I was preaching in one of the smaller villages, some soldiers came to the church, stopped my preaching and forced most of the villagers and me to carry their bags. We carried their bags as forced labor for the whole day. At night, while the soldiers were sleeping, I ran away and escaped from them. I had to flee my country with my family shortly thereafter.

My wife and I stay in this refugee camp now. We live in house number 576 in Section B. We don't get any rations because we are new refugees. We are waiting for their paperwork. Therefore, we have to buy rice, oil, salt, food, etc without an income.

We have a lot of free time here. So we learn English speaking, computers and other languages. I am a student here and also a teacher at the Ethnic Training Center. My wife is an editor of the school newspaper at our school in the camp. She is also a teacher in the Ethnic Training Center. But we are volunteer teachers.

We are so happy for our jobs. We can share our technology to students.

We don't like the refugee camp's weather. It is always raining all the time. Everything is wet. Everything is muddy.

Also, we don't have electric light. We always have to use candles every night.

Ning Kee and his wife's story is fairly typical for the Chin that I met in the camps. They did not flee from a war zone, which is common for other ethnicities in Burma, and they did not flee because they were involved in either the 1988 or 2007 protests, which is common for the majority of Bamar people in the camp. Instead they left their homeland to escape human rights abuses, specifically forced labor and religious persecution.

In this case, Ning Kee and his parish had to porter weapons and other military gear for a company of soldiers dispatched to the India-Burma border area where he had his church. Ning Kee was adamant that the reason the Burmese soldiers chose to use their labor was that they were Christian. Otherwise he said why did they not choose to use the next village over who were Buddhist to work for them.

He said that he was just going to move out of that area after the incident, but after talking to relatives who had already fled similar abuses and had been resettled in America already, he chose to take his family out of the country entirely.

When he described travelling across the country from the north of Chin State to the south of Karen (Kayin) State (see map), he said he had been worried, because the name on the documents he was carrying was obviously Chin. It seems that enough Chin have been leaving their homeland to arouse suspicions of the military checkpoints within the country. Ning Kee and his family, however, were able to make it to Karen State and across the border into Thailand without incident.

* * *

The Radio Operator

My name is Nang Charm Tong. I was born in 1957 at the capital city of Shan State in Burma. I am the third of four sisters in our family. Both of my parents passed away while I was not at home. I feel very sad because I didn't get a chance to see them.

After I finished my high school exam, I secretly left home with a group of school mates and joined the Shan State Army (SSA) in Northern Shan State in 1976. Some of my army friends died sacrificing their lives for our motherland. After completing basic training I became a wireless radio operator. Sometimes, I also had to help our health workers, nurse the sick and the wounded.

I was married with one of our comrades in the same unit in 1988. I had one son with him. When the rest of the SSA signed a peace agreement with the military government my husband refused and his group remained underground.

My husband died in 1994 while fighting with the junta government's State Peace Development Council (SPDC) in a battle. I wasn't even allowed to see his body after that. My life was so difficult in the jungle and I have had to struggle for more than twenty years. I sent my son to my sister to take care of him.

Now I'm alone in this refugee camp. I do not know what bad things may happen to me next. Till now my life is not very stable yet. Anyway, I always hope for the best in the future.

Nang Charm Tong was very demur. I was surprised when I learnt more about her past. I never would have thought of her being a soldier unless she had written this essay. By the time that she had made it into the camps, she was already over fifty.

She looked about twenty years younger.

She was only one of a few Shan people that I knew in the camps. But because her grandmother was from Kachin State, father north of Shan State (see map), she was able to use this as evidence that she was not Shan but of a Kachin ethnicity. Otherwise, the Thai authorities probably would not have let her stay.

In the essay she mentioned that the Shan State Army signed a peace treaty with the military junta. What she is describing is the splitting up of the SSA into two parts: SSA North and SSA South. The northern forces of SSA ended up signing a ceasefire agreement with the government in 1989. Many Shan like Nang Charm Ting's husband were not ready to give up the fight for independence. These fighters banded together in a few different groups, the largest of which was the SSA South. Today, when media reports on the continued fighting between the SSA and the SPDC, unless otherwise mentioned specifically, they mean the SSA South.

Nang Charm Tong did not stay long in the camps. After writing this account of her past, she left a few weeks later to return to Shan State. None of her classmates in the refugee camp have heard from after that.

* * *

The Shop Owner's Wife

I am Sandar Win. I passed the university entrance examination in 1995. However, I forwent university at that time to become a primary school teacher in my hometown in Rakhine State. I was very happy and proud of myself at that time. Then I started a distance education, majoring in geography. I graduated in 2002. However, after I graduated I changed my career again and opened a cosmetics shop.

I met my future husband in 2001 and after one year we married. I had two children. We later moved 200 miles away from my hometown to work in another town. I closed my shop to work with my husband there for five years. We had money problems so I left my children with my grandmother. Sometimes, I missed my children, but I had to get money for my family. I know their grandmother liked to have them around though.

When my children came back to me I was happy, and we lived happily like that together for a while. But in 2005 we had to run away from our country to the Thai-Burma border. This was because the Military Government started to harass my husband at work. They wanted a percentage of his business or they would shut him down. He refused, so we fled. We came to this refugee camp in 2006.

We miss our country and want to go back. Life is difficult here in the camp. But we have no chance. Therefore, we are not very happy, but we must live here because it's too dangerous back home.

Presently, our life is very simple. I have live with my children and husband in this refugee camp in my hut. Normally, I go to the market three times a week. There are butchers', fruit shops and green-grocers at the market. The meat here is cheaper than other places.

The roads here are very muddy and not easy to walk on. Sometimes, I slip on the muddy road. The weather is so cold and it is raining all the times. Rarely do I get to see the sunshine. It is so difficult to dry the wet clothes because of the rain. The misty mountains are very nice looking though, like a picture.

We get water from a pipe from the river; it is brown color with rubbish. The education and training programs are good. It makes it easier to live here. But honestly, living in this refugee camp is bitterly disappointing. But I try my best to live a happy life and struggle for better times in my life.

Sandar Win and her family have been living in the camps for going on six years now. Both she and her husband would attend my classes.

I wondered if it was normal for the local military government to ask for a cut of a small shop owner's business with the threat of shutting one's business down. To me it sounded like something the mafia would do. Sandar Win's husband laughed when I asked, saying that it happened all over Burma. Unless you knew someone higher up in power, there was no way to protect yourself. I asked if it was because he was Arakanese. He said that he thought this was a universal across Burma and not dependent on ethnicity.

Sandar Win and her husband had converted their hut into a small shop selling snacks and drinks. Initially, twenty years ago when the first refugee camps starting cropping up along the border of Burma, the Thai military were not supposed to allow this type of buying and selling in the camps. But today every refugee camp in Thailand has a small market area—a small economy unto itself that ships in goods from other parts of Thailand. Sandar Win said that the shop they ran in the camps was similar to the shop they had had in Rakhine State.

* * *

I come from a very small village with a very small population in Karen State. My name is Lah. My house was nearby a river. I could go swimming in the enormous river. I loved swimming in it. However, my parents didn't let me to go swimming alone, because the river was very dangerous. They said that if I went alone I could drown easily.

I stared to go to school in my village, but I could only go to school for one month, because when my age was five years old, I had to run away from my village with my parents. I was very sad. When the SPDC came they burned everything. I always remember that I had to run away from my village. I hate the SPDC, but I can't do anything but run away. They forced us to run away.

When we arrived in the refugee camp, I was very sad. I didn't have any friends. I was afraid in the camp because the Thai soldiers also had big guns. Maybe they would shoot us too. We heard fighting in the jungle near the refugee camp with big guns and machine guns often at night. I was unhappy all the time. After two or three years, though, I became happy because I found some friends in the camp. This refugee camp is now good for me. But I always miss my village.

Now I live in this refugee camp with hope, because it is safer than Burma. But I don't want to stay here too long, because I haven't got any work or any income. But that is okay; I think that I will have to stay here for another year.

I am happy when I attend school. I meet many friends and learn skills and English. I am interested in listening to my teacher's pronunciation, so I don't want to be absent from school.

I also attend the Ethnic Training Centre, too. I study Karen literature. Karen is my mother tongue. I try to be careful to remember my mother language to preserve it. I know that our ethnicity will lose our culture if we don't learn our literature. Thus, I am also studying my first language.

I do not really have free time on the weekends either, because I go to our church. So I am always helping them for activities. I am happy when I go to church, but sometimes I miss my native land.

I think I will have a shimmering future in the USA.

Because I will have many chances to try as much as I can. And I think I will get an interesting career such as a teacher. I want to accomplish my goals: firstly, I ought to complete my skills, because there will be many good applicants in the US.

If I resettle in the USA, I need to look for a part-time job for my daily expenditures. And I will save any extra money for my education. I will spend a few years getting enough money. During those struggling years, I will attend advanced English courses. And I will attend vocational training school.

I will go to a teacher's college and I will learn about the psychology of children. When I get a degree I will apply for a preschool or primary school. I want to educate all the people, especially in early childhood education.

In my future career, I will build higher skills for myself and will learn more for my education. My career may not be only in America but also in Burma. I will probably go back to my native land someday and will found a school and will be a principal of that school. I want to have a successful career in teaching.

For a Karen, Lah's story of having to flee her village during an attack is common. She was quite young when it happened. After that incident, Lah's family stayed in another village in Karen State for a few years before moving to the refugee camp. By the time she started attending my sessions she had just turned sixteen.

I thought that Lah's English was good for never having been to a normal school, though her accent had an interesting Australian twang to it. She explained that some Australian missionaries had stayed and taught classes in the new village her family had moved to.

She was always very eager to learn and I could see her easily becoming a preschool teacher in the US. At the time of this writing, Lah and her family are waiting to be interviewed by DHS.

The Small Businessman

I am Nol Lar who is at the age of 26. I am joining the English course now and am still waiting for settlement in the United States. I come from Mon State. In Burma I was distinguished and delighted but oppressed and disappointed. Because my parents and two elder sisters were polite, hospitable and educated, they taught me to enjoy this life while I was young. So everybody who saw and met me always loved me.

Because of obeying the teachings of my teachers, my family and grandfather and grandmother, I was clever and kind-hearted and most often got the grade of "A" in elementary school. Whenever I got prizes, I was praised by my Dad and Mum again at my home. That was when I was delighted and satisfied.

Once I felt lost and was depressed when I failed in taking the first exam in grade nine. I felt uneasy about that and my values changed. I disliked studying English and hating subjects taught in that language, but I loved practicing Math. Honestly, at that time I was not interested in education. I also did not abide by the speakings of my parents. However, in grade ten I changed again, so this was an important year in my life. I tried to avoid having bad types of fun, stopped smoking and drinking beer and kept on studying. As a result, I passed grade ten in 1998. It was the happiest day I had ever met.

I had a dream to become a successful businessman in Burma as well as around the world. So I decided to join the University of Yangon. In the other hand, I helped my family's traditional business improve and benefit. As a business student I was encouraged by a teacher who taught statistics to become a sophisticated man. I looked forward to impressing and being loved by beautiful girls. Truthfully, I became a successful and reliable man at the market that was the largest and most famous in Mon State after graduation.

Unfortunately a municipal official in that market reminded the shop owners to give over their employees as forced labor to clean and rebuild the market area. If anyone did not obey the rules, he would punish them by closing their shops and give them a fine of one hundred thousand Kyat [approximately $100 USD]. Because I broke the rules while

I was busy, I tried to avoid being punished and continued to have my employees work for me.

The police looked for me in order to arrest me. They persisted in taking all of the materials from my shop because they could not find me. I could not help my business or employees.

After hearing information of my arrest warrant, I knew I had to run away from Burma. I was determined.

I escaped to Mae Sot, Thailand and it was difficult for me. While I was having trouble in Mae Sot, I had an opportunity to go to Bangkok as a migrant worker. Going through the jungles to Bangkok, I had difficulty eating, staying and walking. I did not have enough supplies and the Thai authorities tried to seize the group that I was with. They did get us but then let us go by paying a bribe. We went to Bangkok to work for two years.

Unluckily, the Thai boss in Bangkok who supervised me stopped paying me wages at the end. I was sick of it. I sometimes thought that I should have stayed in Burma. That was the most disappointing period that I had to suffer through. I was a refugee and it seemed like no one cared. I had been oppressed by both the military junta in Burma and the boss in Thailand.

However, my friend helped me to enroll at the UN office. I was uncomfortable and destitute and was encouraged to come to the refugee camp. I told my story to the DHS from America and received an official approval letter from them in September 2008. But the head person at the office did not allow me to go because he said that my name Nol Lar was too common and unclear. Many Mon have this name, so maybe I was lying?

I understand now that in life, everyman has two main obligations: first, to his family, his parents and his wife and children; and second, to his people and his country. I believed I could continue my obligation and dream in the US, but now I do not know what the future holds for me.

Nol Lar was good-natured and easy to talk to. He also tended to embellish some things, including information about his past. He had two other good male friends that attended these English sessions with him. They formed a group, each around twenty-five or twenty-six years old. Whenever Nol Lar would stand up to talk in class, his mates would always josh him, saying that he was just bragging. I wondered how much of his story was accurate and how much was embellishment. Both of Nol Lar's friends attested that Nol Lar was not so successful a businessman in Mon State as he liked to think. But that he refused to follow the dictates of the local military government was true.

Sometimes the line between migrant laborer and refugee can be blurred. Nol Lar's essay demonstrates this. A human rights perspective justifies his exodus from Burma: he resisted forced labor for his employees. However, a Thai government perspective maintains he broke the law: first in his country by avoiding municipal regulations, then in Thailand by entering and working illegally. It is probably this reason more than any other that the Thai government is wary of allowing people to cross over from Burma. In most instances, by choosing to work and not claiming asylum immediately, Nol Lar was forfeiting the opportunity to live in the camps. I do not exactly know how he was able to gain admission, but he was very fortunate to have had a friend to help guide him through the UNHCR enrollment process and be considered a refugee.

After failing the DHS interview, Nol Lar was still confident that he would make it to the US someday. He can reapply with DHS, but there is no guarantee that they will interview him again.

* * *

The Hostel Owner

My name is Tin Maung. I was born in 1973. I lived in one same quarter of a small town in Chin State. I finished my elementary school in my home town. After that, I continued my learning at a seminary in Maymyo from the seventh to the tenth grades and finished my 10th Standard in 1990. Then I returned to my hometown because my father needed help with his business and he had bad health. I never attended university.

In 1990, December, I went to the land where there is a lot of jade in Kachin State and worked there until 1994. I returned to buy a bungalow for my family, then in 1996 I went to Mogok Ruby Land and worked there until 2003. Because of my experience in gem trading, I started trade between Myanmar and India. I did this until 2004, but then retired from the trade because the profit margin was very low.

At the end of 2004 I built a small hut in a village at the border of Myanmar and India. I made my hut just like a small hotel, like a hostel, so that the travelers may rest, eat and buy some things from me sometimes.

However, the soldiers came and often disturbed not only my work but also my guests. They wouldn't pay me for staying at my hostel, and sometimes they even killed my hens or cocks or dogs. So, we had a big quarrel there. After that they destroyed my hut and everything. They then accused me of being a member of the Chin National Army (CNA) and tried to arrest me but I escaped and went to India. I worked there until I tried to go to Malaysia, but couldn't get there. At last, I made it to Mae Sot, Thailand instead and then heard about this refugee camp. So I came here to the refugee camp in the beginning of 2008 and have been here ever since.

Different people have different plans for their future. I also have a future plan. It's to apply to a college where I can major in law. When I was born my parents committed me to God because they wanted me to serve God. At first I had dreams of being the pastor, but now I have decided to learn law and politics to lead and defend politically charged people in Burma because the situation demands it.

Sometimes we say that someone we know is "a square peg in a round hole." This simply means that the person we are talking about is not suited for the job he is doing. He may be a bookkeeper who really wants to be an actor or a mechanic who likes cooking. Unfortunately, many people in the world are "square pegs." They are not doing the kind of work they should be doing for one reason or another. As a result they probably are not a very good worker and certainly are not happy. I want to avoid such a situation.

Making the right plan is very important for our future. I believe that I would not be a "square peg," because I am ethnically Chin, but maybe I have become so because the Burmese government does not accept us. To develop my people and Chin land in Burma and my future I will study law to help those in need the most.

Tin Maung, like all the Chin I met in the camps, was a Christian. When he said that he studied at a seminary in order to complete 10th Standard, I was confused. But what he meant by using the word seminary was that he had studied high school out of a church, not that he had studied theology at a tertiary institution. I later learnt that since there are very few government schools in Chin State of any quality, some parents choose to send their children off to one of the town's churches. In Tin Maung's case, he had ended up completing his high school at one of these church schools far away in Maymyo (about 40 kilometers east of Mandalay) where he had family.

Tin Maung was very eager to study at university since he had never had the chance. He said that he wanted to resettle, preferable to the US. At the time of this writing he was waiting for an interview with DHS.

* * *

The Cleverest Girl

I am Noe and my nationality is Karen. I was born in 1993 in Karen State in the capital. Before I was here in the refugee camp, I was in Burma. When I was in my village in the mountains I was very happy. But one day the Burmese military entered our village and started asking a lot of questions. They then started to arrest villagers for no reason, saying that we had been helping former political prisoners escape over the border to Thailand. They also caught all our chickens and dogs and goats and whatever they wanted and stole and ate them.

All of the villagers were very afraid. Whenever the Burmese military enters our village, they always ask us a lot of questions. Whenever we answer that we don't know, they say we are lying and then they hit the villagers.

There was a war near my villager once. After that occurrence the Burmese military entered my village again. They arrested five people, one of them was a pastor. They killed them all. After that many villagers tried to escape from Burma.

When I was still in Burma we had always had trouble. Sometimes, we couldn't eat. Sometimes, I couldn't sleep very well. We were afraid.

I am now a refugee. I stay and live in this refugee camp in Tak Province in Thailand. I have two elder sisters and one elder brother. I am the youngest in my family. One of my other sisters lives in Yangon with her family. They have an only daughter.

I am very happy to be a daughter of my Dad and Mom, because they are so kind, as well as guides and heroes for me. They never hit or harm us. I think that I am the most clever girl among my siblings. During my free time I like to be alone, but maybe that is not the best way. Sometimes, I need a friend who can listen and share my stories. Now I have two friends in the refugee camp. They are also so kind and honest and I am happy to be with them and love them. They help me with the difficult situations in the camp.

Only when I arrived in this camp did I get the chance to attend classes like this one and other useful courses for myself. I'm ambitious and in the future I want to become a businesswoman. I hope my dreams will come true in the near future.

Noe was very bright and I felt it unfortunate that she had not gotten more schooling before coming to the camps. But what was really striking about her to me was her ubiquity to just about every other teenage girl the world over. Because she was so very normal, the inequality and injustice of her position seemed more pronounced. I realized it is one thing to hear stories of freedom fighters in the jungle or protesting monks in exotic-sounding cities, but it is quite another thing to hear the story of a cheerfully average girl in a disturbing situation.

In the camps, whenever I walked by her parent's hut, they always invited me in for tea. It was at these times more than any other that I was aware of the negative effects of not being able to grow up in a prosperous civil society.

Towards the end of my commitment in the camps, Noe's family decided to move back to Karen State.

* * *

The Badminton Player

My name is Aung Aung. I was born on November 12, 1979 in a small village in Mon State, Burma. My parents had seven offspring, and we survived by farming. I was the fourth child among seven siblings in our family. In 1984, aged five, I began my basic schooling at our village's primary school. In 1989 I finished my primary level and had to give up my studying after the sixth grade.

After I left school, I helped my parents with farming. While I had free time I always hung out in the giant forest beside our village because I was bored with staying at home and jealous with my friends who got a chance to continue their schooling in the middle school in our village of Mon State.

I, unfortunately, was separated and exiled from my loving family, interesting society, and country when the Burmese military authority burned and destroyed our schools, monastery and houses in our village. They invaded and occupied Hongsawatai in the Mon Kingdom. Now, this town (Hongsawatai) is known as Bago City in Bago Division.

After arriving in Thailand I had difficulty getting help trying to receive a comfortable life. However, now, after having registered with the UNHCR, I feel better and I am happy to attend classes and workshops like these.

Now I'm trying to resettle in the USA. I haven't decided what to do in America.

I don't want to be an office worker. I hate the clock-in-and-clock-out system. I like working with numbers, but I don't want to be an accountant. I also hate working in shifts. I want to work under a flextime system.

I have a few cousins in Baltimore, Maryland. One of my cousins founded the badminton club in Baltimore. Two weeks ago he phoned me that he didn't have a coach and he wanted me to be a coach in his club. So I decided to accept his request, because I'm skilled at communicating and also good with people.

If I were there as a coach, I'll let the members know that "practice makes a man perfect" and I'll order them to come to training regularly. I'll point out to them the importance of speed, stamina, strength and strategy and I'll train them to be good at speed, stamina, strength and footwork. I'll teach them new techniques that I had learned from my father. I'll train them to be good at all kinds of strokes. I'll do this job as long as I can, but I will retire when I can't stand on my feet.

I would often see Aung Aung either playing or teaching others how to play badminton. He always carried around his racket stuffed into his backpack. Aung Aung was friendly and—to the amusement of all onlookers—showed me how to play badminton as well. The popularity of badminton in the camps seemed universal. Whenever an aid agency specializing in youth would visit the camps, they always got requests for badminton rackets and birdies. Nets were often made from rope and unused fishing nets. To be any good at badminton in the camps meant instant popularity.

In Aung Aung's essay he mentioned the town of Hongsawatai. This is a point of pride with all non-Bamar ethnicities in Burma: to preserve the ancestral names of their towns and regions. The Mon people are actually one of the oldest tribes of Southeast Asia. Their culture is considered older than the Burmese's, the Thais', and the Khmers'. They once have settlements all along the Chao Phraya River Valley (where Bangkok is now) when their Mon Dvaravati Kingdom of the sixth to eleventh centuries had considerable influence over the region. I found it normal for the Mon to refer to any of their old cities in the Mon way.

At the time of this writing Aung Aung was waiting to be interviewed by DHS.

* * *

The Social Worker

I am Myan Too, who came from a township in southern part of Shan State, Burma. My family was based on farming for our finances. Our family life was very hard but we could survive. Many years ago we escaped fighting in Shan State. We have not been back.

Now I would like to share one part of my last three years as a story with you:

Three years ago, I lived in Chiang Mai, Thailand. I worked with the National Youth Forum (NYF) as a program assistant. I had to deal with many different kinds of nationalities. Also, I loved to live in Chiang Mai because it was the most beautiful place that I have ever lived in. Before I got a job in Chiang Mai, I had done an internship in Bangkok for six months with the Alternative South East Asia Network on Burma (ASEAN Burma).

During my work with NYF, I had to take care of the training part. I had to translate and be an interpreter for other trainers on environmental issues on Burma. At first, I was so scared to be in front of people for my presentations. One of my brothers and teachers encouraged and guided for me to be confident and strong. I had faced a lot of difficulties and stressful situations from my job but I never gave up. Every time when I felt tired I went to the Chiang Mai University (CMU) compound and did exercise for my health.

I loved my work and I liked to live in Chiang Mai, but now I must live in a refugee camp because I was living illegally in Thailand. One day if I have a chance I will go back there and live in Chiang Mai again.

For my future I aim to be a case worker or social worker, maybe with the International Rescue Committee (IRC) or the Overseas Processing Entity (OPE), which is committed to freedom and human rights. My wife believes that my temporary job here in the refugee camp will help me in the future. I have a strong desire to help others, which is how I feel about my current job.

During that time in the future, I will continue my education and get a Bachelor's, which is required for good jobs. Otherwise, I won't have the opportunity to get a higher position. I can't now estimate which level will suit me well, but I have a wish to take the TOEFL test and an English improvement training course in a university for fluent writing and formal speaking. I can speak other languages. I hope that that qualification will help me somehow.

If I graduate, I fancy being an Overseas Processing Manager. With that position, I could travel around the globe and help refugees, especially on the Thai-Burmese border. But I prefer to go to the refugee camps rather than stay in the office as a secretary. Some people think that it is a piece of cake, but actually not. In my experience, I would also require good computer skills as well.

As a social worker, I know that good communication and listing skills are needed. I know that "experience is the best teacher," I should get much experience with that. I want to posses the best interpersonal skills. I will then also be in a position to further develop these skills for my social work. I am joyful that my current job in the camp allows me to liaise with UNHCR and other outside agencies as well.

If I was an Overseas Processing Manager, I will supervise my staff who work under me well and show them all aspects of case management. Weekly, I will review all case forms and create new forms if need be. I will confront any kinds of challenges. I won't let them say anything demeaning to refugees. I will try to make sure that the refugees become self-reliant.

I will try to have monumental achievements in my life. I don't know how many years I have to spend before my achievements come. In the end, I would be ready to get a job in UNHCR and hope for a higher position. That is my dearest hope for the future.

When Myan Too fled fighting between the SSA and the SPDC, he had very few prospects. He said that his wife was pregnant at the time and that he had decided he was not going to let his child be born in a war zone. He was lucky to have a friend at

an NGO in Bangkok, who helped him get a volunteer position. Though he was not paid at first, at least he and his wife could stay in the back office and receive meals. He later used this to help him get a position in Chiang Mai.

I was always curious whenever I met a Shan person in the refugee camps, since the Thai authorities normally did not want them there. Myan Too leveraged his past experiences and friends to help him register with the UNHCR and later find work in the camps. Sometimes aid agencies do use refugees inside the camps as translators or in secretarial positions. These temporary jobs are highly sought after.

Towards the end of my time in the camps, Myan Too and his family had applied to DHS for an interview. There was no word yet whether he would be granted an interview or not.

* * *

The Villager

I am Shwe Hla Oo. My life in the past was very hard. When I was twelve years old, I had to face many problems in my village and struggled with my farming job. I always worked with my parents in the farm. I wanted to study but I didn't have the chance to learn like my friend who lived in the town. Sometimes, I told my parents that I wanted to study in the town, but my parents said that we didn't have enough money if I went to learn in the town.

Unfortunately, the SPDC soldiers came to my village and caught many villagers, using them as forced labor to carry their loads and boxes of bullets. I was very sad when the military came and stayed near my village. At that time we were not allowed to find and shoot animals in the forest because the soldiers might think we were attacking them.

We had to do the soldier's work every day. When a person didn't follow their orders, they would get a punishment. When a nearby town fell under the control of the SPDC, all of the Karen ethic people left their homes and villages and fled to the Thai-Burma border. I also fled from the village to the Thai and Burma border. Some SPDC soldiers killed some of us Karen people in the jungles as we escaped.

At that time, many Karen people were afraid of the SPDC, and they faced many difficulties. We didn't have enough food, medicine and we had to hide in the jungle. The SPDC then burned down my house and village and rice paddy, so we couldn't go back. Now I must live in this refugee camp.

Like the case of another Karen in this collection Shi Mon (pg.79), not long after Shwe Hla Oo wrote this he returned to Burma. Unlike Shi Mon who ended up joining the KNLA to fight the Burmese, Shwe Hla Oo eventually returned once more to

the camps towards the end of my time there. I wondered if he had joined the paramilitary group as well, but he said that he had not. He had only gone back to a safer part of Karen state in order to visit an ageing relative.

He said that he wanted to be resettled. At first I thought that by coming and going as he did from the refugee camp would somehow void his opportunity for resettlement. I soon learnt that since the process takes so long, months can easily pass by without anyone of the case officers even looking at a refugee's file for resettlement. Shwe Hla Oo was also not on the rations list, so from a logistical perspective none of the aid agencies needed to verify his whereabouts.

After returning, Shwe Hla Oo visited the resettlement offices in the camp again. They told him to be patient, that someone was working on his file. He was told to wait until next season before he could expect to receive more information.

Shwe Hla Oo decided to return back to Karen State.

* * *

AFTERWORD

In November 2010, a nationwide election was held in Burma. No reputable organization has recognized the process as free or fair. The United Nations, the United States of America and other Western governments, and even member nations of the Association of South East Asian Nations (ASEAN) to which Burma belongs have all condemned the exercise as fraudulent.

Before polling even began, the military were appointed to approximately thirty percent of seats in both houses of the new bicameral government. Aung San Suu Kyi's party the National League for Democracy (NLD) boycotted the election. When the day for voting came, voter turnout was purported to be as low as twenty percent in some areas. The party backed by the military government, the Union Solidarity and Development Party (USDP), won over eighty percent of seats up for election. There is no illusion that the military still runs the government in Burma.

After being away from the Thai-Burma border for a year, I returned to visit the camps again to collect some additional documentation for this project. The mood in the camps was one of heightened concern for the refugees' immediate future. Days before we arrived, some officials in the Thai government had made public announcements that the temporary refugee camps ought to be closed. Their line of reasoning was that since Burma had a "democratic" government now, the Burmese should be sent back across the border. It is important to remember that Thailand is still struggling to completely free itself from its own recent military coup in September 2006. The nuanced "democracy" favored by some Thai officials is not what the NLD, nor the 8888 generation, nor what the 2007 protesters were fighting for.

This has led to a nervous unrest for the people living in the camps along the Thai-Burma border. As I left, everyone that I talked to was taking stock of their situation. Most were still hoping for help from the international community.

ACRONYMS

8888	August 8th, 1988
AA	Arakanese Army
AAPP	Assistance Association of Political Prisoners
ACL	America Center Library, Burma
ACP	Arakan Communist Party
AI	Amnesty International
AIO	Arakan Independence Organization
ALD	Arakan League for Democracy
ALP	Arakan Liberation Party
AMI	Aide Médicale Internationale
ANLP	Arakan National Liberation Party
ARC	American Refugee Committee
ASEAN	Association of Southeast Asian Nations
ASEAN-B	Alternative Southeast Asia Network on Burma
BSPP	Burma Socialist Program Party
BVP	Burma Volunteer Program
CMU	Chiang Mai University, Thailand
CNA	Chin National Army
CNF	Chin National Front
DHS	Department of Homeland Security, USA
DVB	Democratic Voice of Burma
ERI	Earth Rights International
ESL	English as a Second Language
GED	General Education Development
HRW	Human Rights Watch
ILO	International Labor Organization
IRC	International Rescue Committee
KNDO	Karen National Defense Organization
KNLA	Karen National Liberation Army
KNU	Karen National Union
LDC	Least Developed Country
MNDAA	Myanmar National Democratic Alliance Army
MNLF	Mon National Liberation Front
MNP	Mon Peoples Front
MOI	Thai Ministry of Interior
MSKA	Moon Shade Kawina Association, Burma
NGO	Nongovernmental Organization
NLD	National League for Democracy
NMSP	New Mon State Party
NYF	National Youth Foundation

OPE	Overseas Processing Entity
PLHA	People Living with HIV / AIDs
RTG	Royal Thai Government
SLORC	State Law and Order Restoration Council
SPDC	State Peace and Development Council
SSA	Shan State Army
TBBC	Thai Burma Border Commission
TNP	Tribal National Party, Arakanese
TOEFL	Test of English as a Foreign Language
UN	United Nations
UNHCR	United Nations High Council for Refugees
US (USA)	United States of America
VOA	Voice of America

ABOUT THE EDITORS

T F Rhoden is on his seventh year in Southeast Asia, but he will return stateside to work on his PhD at Northern Illinois University in fall 2011. He is a graduate of Thunderbird School of Global Management (MBA) and Webster University Thailand (BA, Management) and a former Peace Corps Volunteer. Material for this project mainly came from his experience living and working in a Burmese refugee camp for one year, facilitated by the Burma Volunteer Program. Visit at *www.tfrhoden.com*.

T L S Rhoden has twenty years of international experience and currently resides in Western Europe. He is a graduate of Wirtschaftsuniversität Wien (MBA) and University of Maryland, Schwäbisch Gmünd (BA, International Relations) and a former Non-Commissioned Officer in the US Army. He currently owns and operates a management consultancy out of Germany. Visit at *www.tlsrhoden.com*.

For the multimedia component of *Burmese Refugees, Letters from the Thai-Burma Border*—with footage and interviews taken directly from the camps, and with additional information about how to increase awareness and other issues covered in this project—visit the following website at *www.burmese-refugees.com*.

The editor's own experience in the camps was facilitated by the Burma Volunteer Program (BVP). To learn more about the program or about how you can get involved yourself visit *www.burmavolunteers.org*.

Made in the USA
San Bernardino, CA
21 September 2014